Michael

Michael

The story of a young Christian musician by

MARGARET ANN JAMES

Illustrated

by

Paul Jones NDD FRSA

"All his soul with music offered"

George Mann Publications

George Mann Publications
Easton, Winchester,
Hampshire SO21 1ES
01962 779944

First published by George Mann Publications 1997
Copyright © Margaret James 1997
Illustrations copyright © Paul Jones 1997

A CIP catalogue record for this book
is available from the British Library

ISBN 0-95-244241-8

April 1997

This book is dedicated to all those
who devote their lives to music

*The Sanctuary Knocker
Durham Cathedral*

CONTENTS

Acknowledgements

I wish to express gratitude for the encouragement, love, and support given by Edmund and Katharine Buxton and my husband, Ray.

The book is affectionately illustrated by Paul Jones NDD FRSA, a Dorset Artist, whose drawings and cover design capture the essence of the narrative.

Family letters printed with kind permission of Jean and Duane Ward.

Letter and Funeral address printed by kind permission of Martin and Judith Marriot.

Frederick Pitfield for use of The Michael James Music Trust organ logo drawing.

Extracts from *The Alternative Service Book 1980* is © The Central Board of Finance of the Church of England and is reproduced by permission.

Extracts from *The Book of Common Prayer*, the rights in which are vested in the Crown, are reproduced by permission of the Crown's Patentee, Cambridge University Press.

Extract from The Very Reverend Michael Stancliffe's article printed by kind permission of the literary executors of Michael Stancliffe.

Evening Echo review of 26 March 1980, and back cover photograph of Margaret James reproduced courtesy of the Editor.

Extracts from *A Conductor's Progress*, Tatler and Bystander (3 February 1965) by kind permission of The Illustrated London News Group.

Extract from the foreword of *In My Father's House*, by Corrie ten Boom, (copyright © 1976 by Corrie ten Boom and Carole C. Carlson) reproduced by permission of Hodder and Stoughton Limited.

Permission for the use of a drawing of The Sanctuary Knocker at Durham Cathedral, by permission of the Dean and Chapter of Durham.

Extract from *The Shell Guide to Wiltshire* is reproduced by kind permission of Shell U.K. Limited.

Extract from The Jersey Evening Post, 1967, by kind permission of the Editor.

Extract from The Western Gazette by kind permission of the Editor.

Foreword

I began this book in a welter of mixed emotions. Michael had recently died and we were overwhelmed by grief but still bathed in the afterglow of that greatest of experiences.

We had seen his faith, courage and acceptance in facing his own death, but we were beginning to feel the enormity of our loss. A loss that was difficult to comprehend.

Our friends and relations seemed to place themselves into three distinct categories. The first group would have liked to talk to us but were unable to think of things to say. The second actually tried to avoid us because they felt self-conscious and embarrassed. The third group went out of their way to be close to us, to listen, to talk if need be, or just share their sense of love. At many times we had to be the strong ones.

Michael's life had turned full circle. We had brought him into the world and we watched over him while he died. My great need was to immediately write of the previous few months, much later, with the help of letters and diaries, but above all with abiding memories, I began chapter one.

It has been a fulfilling task to focus my thoughts on to the paper, to pour out my heart at times, to weep and to laugh, in the hope that the reader will find consolation and be able to share in the wealth of our treasures.

We thank God for them and for the thirty years we were given with him. We thank Him for the gift of Michael in the first place and for the knowledge that he is under the shadow of His wing, 'Enfolded in Love'.

Margaret James ~ March 1997

Introduction

Music was a very significant part of Michael's life, and two influential people in his life were renowned organist Dame Gillian Weir, and Barry Ferguson, retired Organist and Choir Master of Rochester Cathedral.

Dame Gillian writes:

> *I have been greatly moved to read this loving account of the life of Michael James. It is clear that he deeply touched the hearts of many people.*
>
> *It was in music that I knew him, when he was a student eager to explore all that its world could offer him; now through this memoir I have come to know more of his accomplishments, his resolve, his struggles.*
>
> *I know that he will have felt the consoling power of music he loved so much as, clearly, did the poet Robert Herrick - let these words, from his poem 'To Music, to Becalm his Fever', speak for Michael and for us:*
>
> > *Fall on me like silent dew,*
> >
> > *. . . . .*
> >
> > *Melt, melt my pains,*
> > *Why thy soft strains;*
> > *That having ease me given,*
> > *with full delight*
> > *I leave this light;*
> > *And take my flight*
> > *for Heaven.*
>
>

Dame Gillian Weir ~ October 1996

Barry Ferguson observes:

This honest and remarkable book about the young Christian musician Michael James reminds us all how to live and how to die: close to God. What more could one ask of a book?

It is a story that makes you smile, that makes you cry, and that makes you grateful. Joy is everywhere.

"Isn't it nice to be alive!", he said at the age of five, after his first day at school.

Pain is here too, in the final stage of his life, but softened and transfigured by his unshakeable faith in God:

"God is here with me and is seeing me through every minute of the day", he said, shortly before undergoing radiotherapy treatment.

Michael - gentle, loving, thoughtful Michael - or even ardent, young and trim (Thomas Hardy's description of another Dorset church musician might seem to fit!) - Michael the performer, the conductor, the teacher, the man, was an inspiration to all who knew him. Through his mother's vivid account his example is likely to inspire many more people.

Barry Ferguson ~ December 1996

Dorset Street

Michael was born on April 13th 1951. I had an uneventful and healthy pregnancy, so it was quite a shock to be in labour so long, all the previous night and until 3.15 in the afternoon. I had barely time to ask if he was alright, complete and perfect, before I fell asleep exhausted, so that we saw him for the first time, together, and knew without doubt his name should be Michael.

Telephoning to family and friends, Ray said, "Unto us a son is given."

From the beginning he was placid and happy, he lay in my arms throughout most of his Christening day with his hands folded and looked up at the Reverend Edmund Buxton, who was also his Godfather, with smiles of contentment. He seemed to be God's child from those first days of awareness, from walking at ten months, talking at a year, singing songs with us, not only nursery rhymes but 'rounds'. He had a sweet nature and was hardly ever naughty.

We took him all over London showing him the famous sights and buildings; he seemed to enjoy it all with a deep interest, asking questions and making comments of his own in long conversations at the age of three. It was a source of amazement and much amusement to onlookers, friends or passers-by to see the depth of conversation from one so small.

We used to travel to Bristol quite frequently to visit Ray's parents on the *Bristolian*. The train from Paddington left every morning at 8.30 a.m. We always went straight to the dining car to have breakfast. The staff were happy to see us and gave us a royal welcome and excellent service. During the journey they came along and asked Michael how he was, what he had been doing and if he was enjoying his breakfast? In return he wanted to know how many trips they would make that day, all about the food, the passengers, the carriages, the engine, the ticket collector and the driver?

It was from that time surely that the love of trains, the magic of steam, and the need for his own 00 gauge set was born. He had a model railway around his bedroom on shelves, complete with scenery and all the accessories one would expect to see on platform and the track.

In later years, he would walk the branch line from Wareham to Swanage, visiting the signal boxes en route, drawing the stations or engine sheds and preparing a model layout of it all. He had a passion for railways and many of his friends were friends because they shared the same passion.

One London day out, Ray took him to Southwark Cathedral and just as they walked through the door, the organ sounded forth in gigantic deep roars. Michael froze and seemed disturbed and excited; the emotion was evidently too much for them to stay more than a few minutes, but it was a momentous day.

Sometimes, he was asked by a kindly adult, "What are you going to be when you grow up?"

"A vicar," was the reply, but as time went by his answer was, "An organist". It was not surprising that he might be musical for we had all the arts represented in both our families.

Ray had spent a time at art college after completing his education as a chorister. My mother and father were both very musical, my brother became a well-known violinist and my sister followed her artistic bent in tapestry and embroidery. I had been a professional actor from the age of twelve. I had hardly ever been out of work in London's West End theatres, in films, radio and television.

Ray and I had met in the theatre world, but his work evolved into production, direction and teaching of television techniques. He organised and managed a small television studio off Drury Lane and introduced and taught television studies at the Guildhall School of Music and Drama.

I continued to work after Michael was born, we were able to ensure that one of us was always at home. On rare occasions my mother came to stay. Michael sat beside me on the settee one teatime whilst we watched a recording of one of my plays for Children's television. He kept looking at the screen and then at me puzzling how I could possibly be in two places at once.

I began to realise that I couldn't do two things well. I had reached the top of my particular tree in starring roles, my dedication to my work in the theatre had to be wholehearted, but now I needed to be a full time mother. I completed a television six week serial, the story of Louis Pasteur, the famous scientist in which I played Madame Pasteur from the age of seventeen to the age of seventy and then I decided to retire. It was the right time, for since I have wondered how I would have coped with all that actresses have to be prepared to do nowadays. We left certain things to an audiences imagination, we were in the business of lifting spirits not wallowing in the seamy side of life.

But every Christmas for thirty years Ray was employed as a Dialogue Director for Tom Arnold's Ice shows. They were the greatest spectacular shows of their time, at the Wembley Arena. Our Christmases were planned around the rehearsals and the three shows on Boxing Day, playing to capacity houses of twenty one thousand happy customers. Ray often mentioned that it was the exciting contrast between the detailed technical work of the television studio and small screen and the broader, full scale production of those vast shows that were so attractive. He loved every moment.

Michael went to nursery school when he was four. It was a school run by the Tavistock Clinic to allow students of psychology to watch normal children at play. He went on two or three mornings a week to Dickens House at the top of Marylebone High Street. It had a lovely garden at the back filled with climbing frame, slides and other useful equipment with its high brick wall keeping out the noise of the traffic and from there one caught a glimpse of the roofs of the Royal Academy of Music.

Michael could read by this time, so often read little stories to the others. They painted with brushes on huge sheets of paper and with their fingers on smaller pieces, very often on themselves, too! There was sand and water, pots and pans and every possible item to keep them amused and learning. Whilst they were thus engaged the students sat round the edge of the room watching and taking notes, sometimes they were drawn into the activities.

One day Ray arrived to collect Michael and found that all the children – eight of them – were washing a young man's hair. He did have a towel round his shoulders but water and soap were being poured over his head in solemn enjoyment of a task being well done. We often wondered what was written in the notebooks that morning and of what psychological importance it was!

He began learning the piano at five, when he started at a little private school in the next road from us, Gloucester Place which runs parallel to Baker Street.

We lived in a flat in Dorset Street, a turning off Baker Street. The flat was upside down and, by that, I mean we went downstairs to bed and upstairs to the sitting room and kitchen. There were rather a lot of stairs both outside and inside the flat. Our front door was on the second floor, then there was a flight of stairs to our bedrooms and bathroom, and a further flight leading to the roof of the world, or so it seemed, to our sitting room and kitchen. Our views were roofs and chimney pots and distant buildings and the delightful sight of the traffic below. There was always something to see from our windows.

We had moved in on our wedding night expecting to stay for six months and instead we stayed for twenty-one years! So the memories of looking down from those windows are legion.

To begin with, of course, we took Michael to school but I can remember him later walking along to the traffic lights and crossing over and seeing us look from the window and excitedly waving, once, doffing his cap in a mock chivalrous way.

I wrote in my diary on September 18th 1956:

> *Michael's first day at school, a day of excitement for all three of us. He looks so grown up in his uniform, brown blazer with a badge on the pocket, 'Follow the Best and Serve'.*

Breakfast gave me indigestion and Ray didn't eat much, but Michael had cereal, scrambled egg on toast and milk, just as usual. He wiped his mouth, discarded his apron and said, "Is it time to go?"

We left in very good time. Ray watched us from the window, giving us a last wave as we turned the corner just a few yards from the school steps. Mothers and children were arriving from all directions.

In we walked and after a moment a teacher came forward saying, "Oh! you're new aren't you? – you as well," to another brown clad infant. Michael let go of my hand with alacrity, "Cheerio," he said and off trotted the trio inside. I waited a moment there feeling as though I had been left high and dry. I heard him answer the teacher with a clear and high pitched "Michael Robert James". I came away a bit wobbly at the knees. Ray and I spent the morning wondering how he was getting on.

I couldn't settle to do anything very much and when 12.15 came I was back at the school.

The hall was crowded with waiting mothers and one could tell quite clearly who the new ones were, because of the sense of anxiety on their faces. In a moment a solemn procession descended the stairs on tiptoe with the teacher's hand upraised. The older children were still working and mustn't be disturbed. Michael came into view, one hand trailing the banister rail. He saw me at once and a beaming smile shone all over his face, then we were out in the street and walking home.

During lunch he told us quite a lot about the morning. There were twenty-four children in his class, the upper kindergarten, twelve boys and twelve girls. There was a 'hook' room with pegs and boxes for shoes. They had games with the piano, sang songs and a hymn.

"I conducted the class for one of the songs," said Michael. "Everyone stood in a circle and I conducted them."

"Did the teacher ask you to do so?" asked Ray.

"Oh no, I just thought I'd do it," was the reply.

They drank milk from little bottles with a straw, had a very short rest and then did some drawing – a train, of course, with FROM MICHAEL on the back. At the end of lunch he looked at us both with a wonderful smile and declared, "Isn't it nice to be alive!"

I wrote in my diary that night,
> *How my love for him wells up inside me! I'm filled with wonder at the little boy Ray and I have been given.*

The next few days were full of surprises and joy and laughter. They began 'real work' as he said, and he was given a star for writing a line of A's thus – aaaaaaa. The joining up of letters immediately seems unusual. For numbers some sums were set: $1 + 0 =$, $2 + 0 =$, $3 + 0 =$, even $0 + 0$. Michael thought that was funny.

Towards the end of the first week, after lunch, he didn't want to go back.

"I want to play with my train," he explained, "and we might have to sit down again and do some numbers and things."

I jollied him along the road saying that as he only went back two afternoons, Tuesdays and Thursdays, he might as well go this afternoon for tomorrow was Friday and then from 12.15 he would have a long holiday until Monday. He agreed with this and was quite happy going into school.

I heard Miss Valerie say, "You can keep your blazers on, we are going to the Park." I came away glad! He was going to be spared 'sitting down' again.

At 3.30 they were back, having walked in a crocodile, a great thrill!

"I walked with Jacqueline," he said. "She wears glasses and can't see awfully well so I held her hand. We picked dandelions and blew the clocks. One of the boys said they are made of poison, but it isn't true!"

The first week had been a success. In one lesson they had to fit the right captions to the set of pictures:– a cat, a horse, a dog, a pig. There were four ticks. He told us he'd had more stars for sums and his reading book was called, *Old Dan the Farmer*. There were empty spaces on each page for a drawing.

"Old Dan is moving so I drew a lorry and put 'removal lorry' on the side."

"How did you write removal?" I asked.

"RUMOVL", he replied.

A boy called Mark brought his rabbit one morning, a grey Chinchilla, which was a great source of delight to the class and indeed, to the rest of the school. Michael said each form took it in turns to come in and see the rabbit in its basket. He had more stars for sums. It was quite some time before we realised that what Michael thought were stars were, in fact, crosses!

Special scissors were used one afternoon. Miss Valerie drew a large tree on a big sheet of paper and the children had small sheets of green, brown, orange and yellow sticky backed paper. They all cut leaves and stuck them on the tree and as though they were falling off and lying on the ground underneath.

He began to show signs of tiredness at the end of the week and had a good howl which relieved the tension somewhat. We've always found that a good cry sometimes works wonders and after it he would be his normal sweet and charming self. He told a little girl at school one day when she was shedding tears, "Don't worry, you'll feel better in a minute."

I believe that going to school is the nicest thing that ever happened to him. That night as he was dropping off to sleep he murmured, "Isn't it lovely! I still can't believe it's true!"

After his bath he was standing on the stool by the basin, just about to clean his teeth. The mirror was covered in steam. I took a cloth, wiped a clear space in the centre and, as his face came into sight, he exclaimed, "The appearance of Michael James." Another bath night, he said, "Aren't my toes getting big! They will soon begin to bloom!"

Wet days, warm days, no matter what, we were out and about. The park was ten minutes walk away. Bus rides in the rain to the museums, boat-trips on the river to the Tower or Greenwich, or shopping.

The Fire Station was just around the corner from the flat. Sometimes the doors were open and we stood to watch the firemen polishing the brasses, or occasionally slide down the pole from the room upstairs. Sometimes the engines roared into life with clanging bells, coming out slowly but soon speeding up the road.

When Michael was about two he shut himself into the upstairs little toilet on our top floor. For twenty minutes I tried patiently to get him to push the bolt back, sounding unworried and as nonchalant as I could, but he began to panic so I rang the Fire Brigade and told them what had happened. I had no sooner put the phone down when the bells started ringing round the corner at the Station and up came an engine to the front door.

Michael, hearing the bells, pushed back the bolt and came running over to the window to see. I picked him up in my arms and ran down the four flights of stairs to the street door. Two firemen stood there in helmets, greatcoats and boots with hatchets in their hands.

"Where is the child that's trapped," one asked.

"Here," I said. "I'm afraid he has managed to get out after all. He heard your bells and came running to see the engine. I'm so sorry to have troubled you."

"That's alright," he said smiling broadly, "but I'd like to come and have a look at the situation."

"Of course!" I led the way.

Michael's eyes were popping out with excitement. The two men inspected the toilet and its tiny window, then the door.

"I should remove the bolt now, Madam," one said.

I assured them that I would ask my husband to do so as soon as he came in. They went back down the stairs and we watched them from the window. A crowd had collected on the pavement, looking up for the smoke, but the engine turned and went home. All was well.

One of Michael's great joys was his blue pedal car. He 'drove' it up to Regents Park whenever the weather was suitable. Ray carried his walking stick to hook the back of the car up or down the kerbs.

To look at the traffic and the amount of pedestrians nowadays you would not think such expeditions were possible, but, in the fifties, it was still comparatively easy to cross the Marylebone Road at the traffic lights and even to be slow about it. The pavements were empty except on Saturdays perhaps and, of course, once in the Park, there were long walks with few people.

He was a born driver. He could manoeuvre into small 'parking' areas, backing, turning, giving hand signals. The joy of it lasted a few years until he was too big to sit in it and his legs too long.

One day Michael asked Ray, "May I learn to play the piano?"

We bought a yacht piano for the flat when we discovered that Miss Stefanie Hilton–Sergeant at the school was prepared to teach him. She taught the children music and movement, known as Dalcroze. She was very kind and full of enthusiasm and Michael learnt quickly.

The little piano only had five octaves, presumably small enough to be used on a yacht? It seemed the right size for our sitting-room but it was obvious after a very short while that he had outgrown it. He would need a full sized piano soon.

We heard of a baby grand to be sold, out at Totteridge near Mill Hill. An elderly lady was moving from her large house to a Home and could not take the piano with her. It was much loved, much played and, if it was going to a good home where it would continue to be loved and played, she would sell it for £25. We saw it and realised it was for us. In fact, we gave her £30.

It was moved to Dorset Street by the removal firm in Baker Street. The van arrived one morning with four men in attendance. They took one look at the stairs, banisters and sharp turns and said, "Can't get up that." Our hearts sank but Ray suggested they fetch the boss from the office.

In a short while he arrived with tape measure and ruler. He measured the widths and heights, then the lengths and pronounced it possible. The men, though sceptical, were ready to have a go! They bet each other half a crown a floor!

In ten minutes they were up on the fourth floor, the legs and pedal foot were then screwed back on, and there was the glory of our baby grand. The men sat around drinking tea, clapping each other on the back, wreathed in smiles and doling out the various half–crowns. Ray's large tip was much appreciated.

We now had two pianos. The sitting–room was rather crowded, but it was great fun for playing duets. We finally had to agree that we should sell the little yacht piano. I have often regretted it as it was such a pretty piece of furniture, besides being a good instrument.

Ray had been a Cathedral chorister as a boy, and Michael's singing voice was so good it seemed obvious he should be a chorister too. Since he was three we had attended St. Peter's, Vere Street on Sunday mornings for the Family Service. It was specially arranged to draw in the youngest children and allow them to understand the service but, at the same time, it was made meaningful for the adults. The Rev. J.T.C.B. Collins was the clergyman who conducted it with the assistance of younger curates from time to time. It was a wonderfully informative experience to develop one's faith alongside the children.

Michael sang in the small choir from seven years old. Ray wanted very much for him to go either to the Chapel Royal Choir or the Temple Church. Both sets of choristers were educated at the City of London School, so we applied to them for auditions. The Chapel Royal was full, but Dr. George Thalben–Ball, the organist at the Temple, wrote to say he would be glad to hear Michael. Accordingly, in the Spring of 1960 we went along to the vestry at Temple.

Dr. Ball was kindly and jovial. Michael sang for him first, *I Vow to Thee my Country*, music by Holst, then sang scales. Dr. Ball played chords asking him to sing the middle note or the bottom or top note. He survived all these tests correctly then had to sit at the piano and play. By this time he had passed Grade IV so he played the pieces he was preparing for the next exam.

Dr. Ball was beaming and turned to me to say, "I think he is just the boy we are looking for. If he passes the entrance exam to the school, Michael can be a probationer here at Temple from September."

We were overjoyed but, of course, the entrance exam to the

City of London was quite a hurdle. In preparation for all this we had asked the school to let him sit the exam the previous year when he was only eight. We guessed he would not have much chance of passing then, but it was what Ray called, 'the opportunity of a dry run'. The Headmaster said afterwards, "Very promising, try again next year."

So for a year Michael went to St. George's School at Mill Hill, a boys' preparatory school, where the whole teaching was geared to more disciplined work. They all seemed eager to learn. He started Latin and French, early science and all the general subjects and his work improved by leaps and bounds.

It was quite an adventure going out to Mill Hill. The 113 bus ran from Baker Street almost to the door of the school. I travelled with Michael the first term, the fare was ls.8d. for me and 10d. for Michael! The journey took nearly three quarters of an hour but it was very interesting and the drivers and conductors got to know us, as did some of the regular customers.

When it came to the time for Michael to travel on his own, I saw him off at Baker Street and met him again at the bus stop in the afternoon. The driver would wave to us as he saw us waiting in the morning soon after 8 a.m. and sometimes the conductor would lean out at the back of the bus and call, "Hallo Michael, come on in lad," and wave a cheery "Good Morning" to me.

Years afterwards, some of the crews were still on the same bus route and, if they happened to see us in Baker Street, would call out and wave a greeting and once stopped the bus, holding up the traffic, whilst the driver had a chat with us.

One particular passenger was a Nun, travelling to a school to teach, from the convent at Mill Hill. She and Michael had great conversations on religious topics and school subjects and I know, because she told me, that when he wasn't on her bus, she was quite disappointed.

The time came for him to sit the entrance exam for the City of London again, shortly after his successful meeting with Dr. Ball at the Temple. The exam took all morning.

I stood on Blackfriars Bridge to watch the river traffic, wandered along the Embankment and thought deeply about this big step we hoped would take place in Michael's life for it seemed exactly the right place for him to be. It was definitely a praying matter. I felt that one o'clock came too soon for me to be able to say all I wanted as I stared at that beautiful City scene, the river bend, the boats, the bridges.

He came out of the playground entrance just as if he had always been there, not a bit awed by the size of the place, though he said he got lost. Finding himself at a large glass door he pushed it gently open and there were 'hundreds of big boys praying!' It turned out to be the Great Hall, with the sixth-formers bent over their desks, intent on their 'A' levels! I can't remember how long we had to wait for the result but, this time, he passed.

The Temple

Being a Temple chorister was a great privilege. The whole of the education of each boy was paid for by the Temple and to be in the strong atmosphere of music and worship, under the guiding hands and genius of Dr. Thalben-Ball, was a very great experience indeed.

A dear friend, Evelyn Hall, wrote of it at the time, and I quote from her article here.

> *There is so much in the very atmosphere of the Temple that is quite remarkable. From the hustle and bustle of London one enters through a small door in the gateway in Fleet Street, into an oasis of beauty, order and great architecture that fortifies the inner resources of the soul. We enter by the porch into the nave of the church, to the left is the 'Round' with effigies of knights on the floor and its lovely pillars.*
>
> *The morning service is celebrated each Sunday at 11.15 am. The conduct of the service is on the old Cathedral*

pattern but on this smaller scale attains an intimacy which is indescribable.

The Master, Canon T. R. Milford, 'Dick' to his friends, is a scholar of great distinction who has in his personality something more of the artist than the ecclesiast. There is the Reader, the Reverend W. D. Kennedy-Bell, head of religious broadcasts at the B.B.C. He is a magnificent Reader. He projects into his First Lesson, reading the significance of the Old Testament records of the perpetual human story, travailing God-wards. The Master's more cerebral habits of speech show a leaning towards contemporary translations of the Scriptures and his sermons have that quality which make one want to have them to read again and study.

But to me it seems the music is THE worship, so triumphant and exultant in some of its parts, with the keenest phrasing and beauty in the quieter passages and psalms. I often meditate on that child who is now singing in the Temple. I notice his shy pride; I see him in contact with his innumerable school-fellows, with wonderful teachers in whose care he is included, and under the guidance of Dr. George Thalben-Ball his music grows. It is a reassuring experience to see the conditioning that is going on in one small child's soul.

In those first few months the Temple, for Michael, was the organ and Dr. Ball. Michael wrote:

When one comes to the first service as the youngest probationer in the choir, one climbs the steep stone steps to the organ loft, a high platform at the side of the church with sound pouring from it, and sits with Dr. Ball on the

*end of the bench watching him play for the service. After
a while, perhaps, one may even pull some stops and feel
as though the great noise is coming from ones own finger-
tips.*

*Then one becomes a chorister and there is a choir stall
view of the organ. Between the pillars are forests of pipes
and behind those, great machinery in command of which
is a small figure, hidden by curtains, who masters the
whole into producing a glorious and wonderful sound.*

An entry in his diary – apropos the first year's experience
at Temple:

*Isn't life wonderful? I think it is the nicest thing that
God invented.*

Going through to the City meant travelling on the Number
13 bus. It only took a quarter of an hour to go right through the
West End at that time of the morning and we arrived at Fleet
Street at 8.45 a.m.

Again, I travelled with Michael for the first term or so but
gradually he did it on his own. He was nine years old, very
sensible, and could be trusted to be sensible on all occasions.
The City of London School was 'safe' and friendly too. We
found the fifth and sixth formers were always ready to help
the younger ones and if there was a little bullying it was very
soon stamped on by the other boys or masters.

Temple boys, there were usually about twenty-two of them
– eighteen singing and four probationers, all walked the few
hundred yards from the school to the church for practices on
Tuesdays and Fridays. Tuesdays were boys only. Fridays were
the long practice, before tea with just the boys. This was

followed by tea with Dr. Ball, who paid for them all at the nearby cafe in Fleet Street, then the men arrived. Usually the practice went on until 8.30, so Fridays were late nights.

Sometimes there was a wedding on the Saturday, maybe a funeral during the week. These were extra pay! Occasionally a record was made and this meant visits to E.M.I. in Abbey Road. Quite frequently the choir broadcast, or a few boys would be needed for a B.B.C. programme. Michael was in many 'Schools' or music programmes and met Benjamin Britten when they were making a recording of his Spring Symphony.

Michael also met Roy Jesson, Professor of Music at the Royal Academy of Music. Roy was accompanying Michael and his choir colleague, Graham, son of Ernest Lough, in a duet from one of the pieces of music Oliver Cromwell asked to be sung after the Civil War, *Gaudent in Coelis* part of Cantica Sacra published in 1662. This was for a record in *The Makers of History* series, with Paul Rogers as Oliver Cromwell. After this we asked Roy Jesson if he would give Michael piano lessons. He heard him play one morning at his flat in Hampstead and agreed to take him on.

It was the beginning of an all too short but happy friendship for only six years later Roy died from a kidney illness at the age of thirty-five. He said that Michael was exceptionally musical. He was a very good teacher and encouraged Michael in all his music making.

During all this time, of course, we had holidays; life was not all work and no play. There were visits to godfather Edmund Buxton who was now vicar of Milborne Port in Dorset. We went every year to Bedfordshire to my Mother's first cousin, Winnie, whom we always called Auntie Winnie, where her husband was the manager of a small farm in Blunham.

Auntie Winnie's Mother was still alive, our Great Aunt Ginnie. She lived with Auntie and Uncle John and their son, Peter. Ginnie was an affectionate name derived from her names, Jane Disney. She was a very old lady but we never saw her hands idle. She was either preparing vegetables or fruit at the kitchen table or sitting in her comfortable chair sewing. She was a prodigious seamstress and made patchwork quilts and cushions. She was still sewing six weeks before she died at the age of ninety-three.

Michael, now eleven, said with sadness that he remembered how soft her skin was, how when he kissed her it seemed as though his kiss would be too hard and would sink right into her cheek. Then he said, "She'll be making patchwork quilts for God now. Oh no, that's too material, they'll be patchwork thoughts."

We also had wonderful holidays at Birling Gap near Beachy Head. We rented a small cottage from the well known Scottish actress, Jean Cadell. She was often there and members of her family too, but it was sometimes empty and Jean was only too glad for it to be used by us.

Birling Gap was quiet, just the sea and the great Seven Sisters Cliffs stretching on either side, a pebbled beach but sand at low tide and the Downs rolling for miles with the sheep often just the other side of the cottage garden fence. The farmer rode across the Downs on his white horse; he could be seen a mile away sometimes on the brow of a hill. They were peaceful and contented holidays.

Wonderfully refreshing breaks from the noise and bustle of

London. We all three used to return renewed in health and spirit especially if, in Michael's early years, we were able to spend three weeks there. A week to wind down – slowly and thoroughly relax, a week to enjoy it to the full, then the last week to begin looking forward to home again. At least, that was how Michael explained it, as he was always eager to get back to the model railway and the piano.

On wet days Ray helped him make a railway from drift wood and gleanings from the beach after high tide. Stations, bridges and embankments, for instance. It was surprising what they could make from toothpaste tubes, cartons and packages of all kinds from the groceries we bought at the village store. In no time at all, Michael would be lying on the floor with a whole imaginary railway network and rolling stock!

The village, a mile inland, East Dean, was completely unspoilt and little altered nowadays for it all belongs to the National Trust. There are miles and miles of Downland walks and cliffs, though some of the Downs have been used to grow corn.

We had an 8mm cine camera and made many films of our holidays, but one particular shot of Michael coming out of the cottage gate, aged four, bucket and spade in hand, stays in my mind. Little grey shorts, tee shirt with zip at the neck, green knitted cardigan swinging, ankle socks and ever that joyous smile. He passes us with confident look and stride, and carries on down through the bent twiggy trees, stunted and bent in one direction from the wind, down through the gorse and blackberry hedges towards the cliff edge, a hundred or so yards beyond. If I can't sleep sometimes at night, I recall that picture and follow the child. I am very often asleep soon after.

We were snowed in there one Easter; we arrived in gorgeous warm sunshine on Easter Day at tea time after all the splendid services in Temple, the music full of the risen Lord! We had brought half a cooked turkey, vegetables, bread and a large piece of Michael's thirteenth birthday cake with us, milk and tea.

In the evening we walked along the beach collecting driftwood for the open fire; it seemed to be turning quite cold by the time we returned to the cottage; we built up a good fire and settled down for an early night.

In the morning the bright light woke us early. Snow lay several feet thick round the cottage where it had drifted and over a foot deep everywhere. We had ordinary good walking shoes with us, but nothing but wellington boots would have sufficed to keep our feet dry in that weather.

We shovelled a path round from the back door to the coal bunker and found a few pieces of coal left there and some coal dust which we packed in paper. Ray was immediately in charge of 'supplies' – he had not been a Boy Scout for nothing – the drift wood was sorted out, the fire kept going and there we remained, not able to get out of the cottage for three days.

The phones were down at first but later we learned that we were completely cut off with high drifts on the roads. It was extremely cold and we used some newspapers to fold into draught strips to seal the windows. Luckily, we found enough fuel for the fire to keep it going day and night.

We put all the beds in a square round the fireplace at night and it was the greatest adventure, though frustrating, not to be able to get out into the snow at all. It would have been far too difficult to dry off wet clothes and shoes.

Our food lasted us well. I made a thick broth with the turkey carcase and vegetables. Cooking was easy on the Calor gas stove with a full supply of Calor gas in store.

On the fourth day we heard from the village that a car could get through to us so accordingly we packed up and prepared to leave, long before we would have returned home had things been normal, but by that time we had quite naturally come to the end of our resources and no-one could tell us when they thought the weather would change.

The car crawled most of the way into Eastbourne where we caught the train back to London. The carriages had the full heating on, we were 'boiled' and hardly knew how to bear such an immediate switch from one extreme to the other. We tried to open windows to let in some good fresh air but to no avail.

Just a short distance from Croydon, we went into ordinary Spring landscape. The snow blanket was left behind; if it hadn't been for Television News, I'm sure no one would have believed us had we told them of our arctic holiday.

Michael enjoyed most things at school; the atmosphere was good and the teaching excellent. He wrote of one of the masters:

> *You know the way Sandersons is such a sumptuous and marvellous shop that you feel you have to buy good things there, well, Mr. Hatton is like that. He is a wonderful teacher that even the boys who don't like History and Geography feel they must do good work for him.*

Only two years later at a half-hour interview with his form master, July 1962, Mr. Hall, known as 'Daddy' Hall by everyone, told us:

He has a scholarly mind; we are all delighted with the results of the term's work and exams; of course, we knew that he would do well. If he goes on like this he should get an English scholarship for Oxford.

He has a good brain and one of his greatest assets is his joy and love for life and learning. He likes words and the sound of them and enjoys our poetry readings and plays which brings out his dramatic qualities.

He will have to learn to live with jealousy – the duffers and silly boys will always be jealous. Not that he will be unpopular but you see Michael is earnest and that isn't always appreciated. He is never naughty, is he! He doesn't want to be, I can see that, but he has a jolly good sense of humour and we can joke with him as though he were an adult, also reason with him in the same way.

He will do big things at this school and, when I have retired, you can write to me and tell me if I'm not right. He'll get a scholarship to University. He's got too good a brain just to be a musician but, of course, a Doctor of Music and his English would be alright!!!!!

Don't let him decide or concentrate on one thing yet. Get him about, widen his horizons and he will continue to do well. He is such a sweet chap and very rewarding. A boy like Michael makes being a teacher worthwhile.

There was always a lot of homework, some more tiresome than others. We used to fortify him with snacks and drinks after supper, and he commented one evening:

After wallowing around in the depths of science you need a glass of milk!

He had been asked to write some epitaphs for pet animals one day and after a while he came into the sitting-room to read the finished products to us:

Here lies my fish
He'd reached the age of seven
He died on June the 8th
Ascended now to heaven.

Billy my cat
Departed this life
On the last day of September
My only cat
My dearest friend
Whom I will e'er remember.

Hatty Hedgehog died October 16th 1960
I'll ne'er forget my prickly pet.

Running parallel with all the work at school was the glorious music at Temple, and the study and development of his own music. This was hard work too, but he loved it all so much there was hardly a moment when he considered it work at all.

His piano repertoire was widening, his chorister's voice was gaining in confidence under Dr. Ball's influence, and his whole musical ability was deepening.

He was given short solos to sing in the services; he stood on Cantoris side; his voice was second treble. In the psalms, Dr. Ball's pointing, the way he rehearsed the boys and the way he conducted the choir in rehearsals was supreme. Every word of the psalms, every phrase was given full meaning. The music was never paramount; the words must come first and the timing of each verse was essential.

After a repeated bad entry during practice one evening Dr. Ball said, "If you want to catch the 2.30 train, you have to be at the station beforehand. It's no good walking onto the platform at 2.31."

On giving meaning to all words in a song he said, "A sprinkling of pepper makes all the difference to the taste of a tomato."

Dr. Ball had many little stories and anecdotes; he was never cross, never angry. He was full of love for the boys. He often said, 'I love my boys,' and it was with this love he produced such a fine choir.

"There could not be a finer choir in the whole of England," was a comment from Dr. Don, a former Dean of Westminster.

After every service Michael went up to the organ loft to turn pages for Dr. Ball's Voluntary. In his diary dated April 15th 1962, he wrote:

> *Dr. Ball had just finished playing Bach's Fugue and Toccata in D Minor and we pushed the stops in. I said, "This is the part I like," and hummed the phrase. "I know what you mean," said Dr. Ball and he made sure that all the stops were in and played the phrase again while we both hummed the tune quietly.*

Michael was confirmed at Temple with four other boys of the choir on May 15th, 1964 by the Bishop of Stepney, Dr. Lunt. It was a beautiful service. My mother sat with us and for the first time for many, many years, took Communion with us afterwards. She told me that at last she felt she could be accepted back into the family of the church after so long. Her father had been a Deacon of Islington Chapel and she had always attended church every week as a child.

With a deep sense of thankfulness we realised that Michael's Confirmation had been responsible for renewing the faith she was to keep until she died. How much her faith had always been below the surface I do not know; I certainly learned my childhood prayers and hymns at her knee.

Michael served for Communion the first time on Christmas Day. Canon Milford said to him "I'm so glad you are going to be with me for the service. What a wonderful day to remember for you, your mother and father and grandmother."

After the service he had to return from the vestry to snuff out the altar candles. He stood beside them with the candles several feet above his head trying to blow them out, then tried putting them out with his fingers, but, of course, they were very large flames. Ray went quickly up and whispered, "Lick your fingers first!". This time the candles were snuffed successfully. The real 'snuffer' was locked in the verger's cupboard!

Michael sang more and more solos; his voice had something of a Cor Anglais tone; he was often complimented on his singing by the choirmen or members of the congregation but it was Dr. Ball's comments which were most satisfying to him; taking it all as just a sign that he was on the right track and all was well.

He took his Grade VII piano exam early in 1965. The music master at school, Dr. Wray, said he'd be very surprised if he did not pass.

He ought to go all out for music now; there are several music scholarships for University; he ought to begin the organ properly; take music for O level first, that's a good start. If he gets a scholarship it would mean reading music only for three years. Thorne (sixth former) got to Christ Church, Oxford last year – he becomes the College organist while he's there.

Dr. Ball gave Michael his first organ music soon after and said he would buy him a book of Bach preludes to start him off. When the results came in for the Grade VII exam he had passed with Distinction, 132 marks out of a possible 150.

Scales and Arpeggios	*21/24*	*All ready touch and rhythm commendable*
Sight Reading	*15/18*	*In musicianly style*
Aural Tests	*17/18*	*Very good*
Handel Variations	*24/27*	*Very musical playing - sensitive in tone quality and he was very alive to tempo in changing from one variation to the next*
Mozart Sonata	*23/27*	*Neat and very musical in style*
Scriabin Prelude	*16/18*	*With a good command of soft and sustained tone. Very sensitive to the mood of this music.*
Strauss Reverie	*16/18*	*Delicate in tone quality, capably handled.*

Remarks: A promising young musician and pianist.

The Master of the Temple, Canon Milford, told Ray one Sunday, "I said to Michael today we are in trouble, no probationers, no collection."

"Don't worry," said Michael, "just leave it to me."

Duly, there were four choirboys selected and organised, Michael being one himself. Then the Master went on to say, "What a paradox to hear the prayer in the Te Deum, *Vouchsafe O Lord, to keep us this day without sin,* sung as a treble solo by one so young, so good and gentle-hearted as Michael."

The Master invited all who'd served for the 8 a.m. Communion service to breakfast in The Master's House next to the church.

These breakfasts were a joy to Michael as they could talk deeply of the Bible and of their faith. He asked as many questions as he liked, Canon Milford could answer them. He spoke to Michael as to another adult in these discussions. Then the talk would change to matters of household importance. "Michael how do you think I could mend the refrigerator handle?" It was obvious that Meccano came in very handy, even for dealing with items that went wrong in the Master's Study!

Mrs. Margaret Milford was a sweet, little lady, bright as a robin, ready at all times to talk to the boys, to comfort troubles and to answer the door to the newest of probationers who had been sent for *The Grimmett* (a sort of corruption of the word grommet – a car part or widget). She would tell him that it was one of the boys' jokes and not to mind. "Come in and have a chocolate! When you go back make sure you tell them how delicious it was!"

A headmaster of a well-known London preparatory school told us once that the combination of the City of London School and the Temple was the finest education a boy could have at that time. This proved true over the next few years.

~·~·~·~·~·~·~·~

Head Boy

The Tatler and Bystander Magazine, priced 2/6d, was published every month and in the February edition in 1965 was an article entitled *A Conductor's Progress*. It was written by Charmian Tate with photographs by Graham Attwood.

They came to the flat to interview Michael and take photographs of him at the piano and also on the floor with his latest Meccano model, a working crane with a jib some two feet long; they chose one at the piano in a characteristic 'thinking' pose, one hand on the keys, the other behind his head with elbow on the front of the music rest.

Charmian Tate analysed the steps that lead from an early urge to wield a baton to the commanding world position held by Sir John Barbirolli:

> *Michael James is fourteen years old and has decided, quite definitely, that he will be a conductor. Such conviction rarely happens so early – though Sir John*

confesses he was only four when he became fascinated by the conductor's white gloves. The first signs are usually an interest in an instrument and Michael was three when he announced he wished to learn the piano. Now he is an accomplished pianist and sings in the Temple Choir. His next stage will be entry to one of the music colleges where he may find a growing interest in other branches of music.

Ian Horsbrugh is studying at the Guildhall School of Music and Drama. His decision to opt for music came late: he was seventeen when he heard his first concert, but that decided him, he is taking a conductor's course and studying the cello and piano. Sir John Barbirolli studied the cello, Colin Davis the clarinet. For college graduates in conducting, the course is perilous. There are few openings in this country, some young conductors find themselves in charge of musicals, others find themselves teaching. The temptation to go abroad is great and Ian Horsbrugh feels he would like to try a spell in America, appreciating the value of a different approach.

James Loughran has one of the few valued jobs available to post graduates, that of assistant conductor of a symphony orchestra, he is with Constantin Silvestri at Bournemouth.

Frank Doolan is currently conducting at Sadler's Wells. He has been on the music staff of the opera house for three years having trained at the Opera School. He studied the violin at the Academy and now takes rehearsals, coaches singers and chorus and prepares scores, even perhaps banging an anvil during Rheingold as the music staff at Covent Garden had to do last year.

Colin Davis at thirty-eight is musical director of Sadler's Wells and is considered this country's greatest conducting hope carving out an individual path for himself by emphasis on Berlioz and Stravinsky. In 1957 he was appointed assistant conductor of the BBC Scottish Orchestra. He never went abroad and feels no necessity to do so. He received a C.B.E. in the New Year Honours List and conducted the first televised concert at the newly opened Festival Hall this week.

Sir John Barbirolli built a considerable reputation for himself as a cellist before turning decisively to conducting when he was twenty-seven and directed three operas (after only three and half hours rehearsal for each) with the English National Opera Company. Ten years later he took over the New York Symphony Orchestra from Toscanini. That was in 1936: in 1943 he became conductor and musical director of the Hallé Orchestra and in his hands it became one of the great orchestras of the world. Lady Barbirolli (oboist Evelyn Rothwell) says that, given four hours, her husband can make any orchestra sound like the Hallé – a process one assumes is happening to the Houston Symphony Orchestra of which he is conductor-in-chief.

Dr. Ball's influence on the music of the Temple Church was considered just as great, following in the tradition of Walford Davies and before him Edward John Hopkins. Visitors to the Temple came from all over the world, 'just to hear the psalms', they said. One could hear each Sunday that the boys were inspired, for the morning Service was an uplifting experience, the music did make the words of the liturgy paramount.

One day at practice, Dr. Ball gave Michael a book of organ music. "Some of it is trash," he said, " but the rest will help with your sight reading."

He also encouraged him to try the Toccata and Fugue in D Minor. Playing it as the Voluntary after Service one morning he turned to Michael in the middle of the Fugue, "You should play this, you know it's not at all difficult."

Dr. Ball gave him many solos as his voice grew stronger and the solo in the Te Deum by Bullivant became Michael's own. There was a pause before the solo, then a deep rumble came from the organ's thirty-two foot pipe, so deep a note it sent vibrations throughout the church, then unaccompanied, *Vouchsafe, O Lord, to keep me this day without sin.*

Dr. told us he thought Michael's voice was beautiful and that a member of the Bench had told him he had never heard a boy's voice like it in all his life and how it filled the church. 'Real professional singing' was his verdict, which was high praise indeed from Dr. Ball.

When the B.B.C. asked Dr. to supply a boy to sing *The Bee-keepers Introit* in a Children's Hour play, *A Swarm in May* by William Mayne, he chose Michael. A few weeks later, the producer, Elizabeth Brown and her programme assistant, technicians and tape recorders arrived at Temple and the recording was made. He was promised a tape of it and a professional fee.

There were many activities for the choir and Michael's Post Office savings book was filling up with entries; there were royalties from records, and extra pay for funerals, memorial services and sometimes weddings.

The deep learning process of this time was very evident, just to be with Dr. was a growing experience, but when during a practice he would explain in a particular way how he wanted something sung, Michael would write it in his diary afterwards.

I was presenting the Introit – "Christ also suffered for us, leaving us an example that we should follow His steps," Dr. Ball said, "Don't make the steps great wide things like those outside St.Paul's," here he stretched wide his arms to emphasize the point, "but like little plodding feet." I tried it and it was perfect – marvellous man!

The entry next to it is about school breaking up for the summer and how the choir boys had to get to Temple for practice during a severe storm:

A wild dashing of boys with bulging cases, flying from shop to shop or door to door. At last all were safe but soaking at Temple having run through a dark sea, ankle deep, under the library entrance. The dark sea had left its mark, for rows of socks hung on the radiators and pools of water were glistening on the floor. Dr. Ball immediately handed out pay, £1 for a broadcast and spirits were revived. Now we could look out on the dark foreboding sky and laugh. The angry storm raged outside but could not get in. By the time practice was over, the storm had slipped away to render its fury elsewhere and the sun glistened from every corner to reassure us.

Every summer the boys went to camp run by two gentlemen of the choir, Mr. Donald Simpson and Mr. David Lewer. Each year they rented a field in the village of Langton Matravers near Swanage, Dorset. David owned a cottage in the High Street so this made an excellent headquarters.

An earlier party of older boys went ahead to set up the camp sometimes, but usually all the gear was on the train and had to be off-loaded onto a lorry at Swanage Station.

The main line train, pulled by a steam engine, brought the boys to Wareham, where they had to change on to the branch line for Swanage, passing Corfe Castle on the way.

The branch line has since closed, but the trackway still exists as a walk. Corfe Castle station, though overgrown, still stands, and Swanage is now the proud possessor of a Steam Train private club. One can travel a few miles up and back on an existing line and buy memorabilia on the station.

The lorry took luggage and boys all the way up the hill to Langton Matravers, a mile and a half away, and for ten days they gloried in the Dorset countryside.

They made visits to the Tilly Whim Caves, to Dancing Ledge, to Kimmeridge Bay and Lulworth Cove, to Poole and maybe a ferry crossing to the Isle of Wight.

They always gave a concert in the church at Langton Matravers each year at which most of the villagers were present. It was looked upon as one of the highlights of their year.

Many 'old' Temple boys turned up during camp to stay either under canvas or at David's cottage and Dr. Ball came down and stayed at a local hotel for a night.

It was a wonderful way to cement the team of boys as a choir, to make them feel they all belonged, and they returned to London full of vigour and ready to take up school work and choir practice again.

Sometimes it rained, of course, but more often than not,

Michael looked as brown as a berry, not only from the sun but from the Dorset air and wind of the Isle of Purbeck.

What days, what balmy beautiful days!

Temple Camp,

Leeson,

Langton, Dorset.

1.9.65

Dear M and D,

Thank you very much for cards and letters. What do you think of the new issue stamp? I had a nice chat with the lady in the Post office about stamps in general and we agreed that these new ones are a bit dull in colour; have you got a block of all the different ones?

In Swanage the meteorological noticeboard states quite correctly that, for the last four days we have had ten hours of sun every day. I have a lovely brown tan, no doubt enhanced by the terrific amount of swimming that I'm doing. The beauty of the heat is that everything dries so quickly, even after that patch of rain last week everything was soon dry.

The concert on Saturday went very well, Peter played the organ with great skill and the audience were very appreciative. The proceeds went to the new vestry fund. Graham sang the solos, Geof and Tony sang alto and I led the boys in endings and beginnings while Dave conducted (a rather erratic beat)! The concert seemed to will good fortune for the weather has, since then, been perfect.

As I write this letter I am sipping some Bulmer's Woodpecker Cider, a bottle of which Simmie so thoughtfully provided for our tent.

Monday evening saw the boys sitting around the camp fire singing songs. We had a whacking good time! The fire was the best yet, with flames at least five feet high and sparks flying into the air. When the youngsters were in bed we started to sing the Banana Boat Song - this year's camp song - very quietly at first then as we got going, louder. It's an old Negro song, sung as they worked a boat load of bananas down the river. Solo: 'As we go down we sing this song'. Full: 'Deo, Deo, I want to go home, etc.' You probably know it. We started to sing around twenty past ten and did not finish until ten to twelve! We worked out that we had sung something in the region of 180 verses! We weren't tired; we just sat and made up verses late into the night, very magical. We were not in bed until 1 o'clock that evening, or perhaps morning!

From the sleeping point of view I have been very warm, snug and comfortable, sleeping solidly right through the night. Food has been very good especially when I am Orderly!! By the way, I have finished the eight pictures on the camera; I'm glad that the photos at your end are O.K.

Must stop now, a card later.
Much love to you both,
Your dear son,
Michael

Dr. asked Michael to be Head Boy in April just after his 15th birthday, this meant that he stood on Decani corner opposite the organ so that he and Dr. could see each other. It was the custom for the Head Boy to conduct all the music with movement of the head, Dr. Ball following. He said that Michael would influence the choir in a big way and it was amazing how much a good Head Boy could do. "He is giving some very fine leading and his solo singing is of the first order."

Canon Milford asked us if we were not proud, he said "I would like to know Michael when he is thirty, that's a wonderful age for a man with his personality, but I don't suppose that I shall be alive then." As it happened he was to outlive Michael by a further four years.

There was a typical description in the diary of being Head Boy:

> *When I sang Cantoris I was just passing the lead on – like a mirror reflecting an image – but now I am the engine pulling a train of trucks and I can feel the weight behind me! If they get slower I have to pull extra hard to climb the gradient. Sometimes 'the train' is going downhill and if the trucks begin to run away I have to hold back and apply the brakes. It is quite a job.*

He stood in front of Ernest Lough and, one Sunday as Michael waited to sing the solo *He was despised* from the Messiah, Ernest leant forward and whispered, "Best of Luck! If you are nervous, I'll do it."

Michael said he could hardly suppress a giggle – an alto solo, sung by a baritone!

Suddenly when the solo was only half way through the organ stopped. Michael carried on and after an interval the organ came in again.

There were congratulations from Dr. afterwards and also from the gentlemen, Mr. Prewer gave him a half crown and Dr. apologised for having 'boobed'.

When we returned home for lunch Michael said that he liked

to stand up and sing and that enjoying singing 'must be the best way to create joy in worship'.

Up in the organ loft the following Sunday Dr. began the Voluntary and in one of the pauses, turned to give Michael a hug saying his verses were lovely, only to finish off the scale after that perfect pause and then at the end of the great St. Anne fugue, "What a big noise! By the way would you like to be with me in the organ loft at Westminster Abbey next week?"

Michael wrote:

August 2nd. I walked round in pouring rain to Deans Yard and went through the gilt gate; on through the cloisters to the small door and steps, which lead to the Nave of the Abbey. Ignoring the notice 'No Entrance for Visitors' I opened the door.

Evensong was in progress but the verger beckoned me over to the steps of the organ loft. I sat next to Dr. Ball who was listening to the service, afterwards we agreed that although it is all very distant there is something good about partaking in thought, while the service continues within the 'Holy of Holies', just listening quietly and meditating.

Then Dr. went up to set the organ and, of course, it had all been changed by Douglas Guest, the resident organist. So there, for twenty minutes, Dr. Ball was pressing buttons to set all his stops, getting flustered without showing it, telling everyone he had not practised the pieces at all, at least, not on this organ!! Martin Ellis turned the music and Ian le Grice and I watched. Miss Jennifer Bate prepared the music; she might be coming to Temple to help Dr. Ball.

At 6.15, 2000 people had taken every available seat but still they came in.

Dr. Ball sat on the stool and said, "Right, stand by for take-off." But the count down was delayed and the yellow light/buzzer went off five minutes late.

"Oh well, here goes," he said, pulled stops and with professional efficiency quite devoid of nerves began to play.

He played superbly with such concentration, beaming at the console. His pedalling technique was fantastic, his use of stops marvellous. At one point, stretching forward to the solo manual, he produced a sound so pleasing to him his face was alive with a childish grin of delight.

I learnt a lot from his playing – a slightly larger but basically the same kind of organ as Temple.

Afterwards, when he had played the last chord Dr. Ball beamed round at us and I do wished we could have clapped. Everyone congratulated him, including Douglas Guest, it was such a success!

It made a marvellous contribution towards the 900th Anniversary celebrations.

In October the terrible Aberfan Disaster occurred, a coal tip suddenly slid down on to a village and buried a school, two hundred children and their teachers died.

On the Sunday afterwards the Temple Service was in progress, we turned towards the altar and began to say The Creed. Every word meant more to me than ever before, I believed every part of it, then suddenly, I saw a crowd of children, high up, floating in a kind of wraith in front of the stained glass windows. When I say I saw children, I mean that I saw the essence of children, their joy, gaiety and happiness, all bubbling, light and frothy, I actually heard them laughing and full of life!

The Creed was coming to an end, the organ seemed louder than usual as I said .... *and life everlasting*. I realised I was seeing the Welsh children, it filled me with such joy I could have shouted aloud, as we knelt to pray I was able to say an immediate Thank You for such a wonderful revelation, I knew I had seen the spirit of life after death. This experience had profound meaning for me ever after. I could never doubt that there was a place prepared for all those that love God.

The collect:

> *O God, who hast prepared a place for them that love Thee, that passeth all man's understanding, pour into our hearts such love toward Thee, that we, loving Thee above all things, may obtain thy promises, which exceed all that we can desire.*

In Corrie ten Boom's book, *In My Father's House*, she writes,

> *Today I know that memories are not the key to the past but to the future. I know that the experiences of our lives, when we let God use them, become the mysteries and perfect preparation for the work He will give us to do.*

The memory of that particular morning in the Temple Church was to prove one of my greatest strengths in 1981.

The choir boys all belonged to the Temple Union after their voices broke but each Head Boy joined earlier and Dr. Ball as the President gave Michael his badge, he said "I've always thought this a very beautiful thing, always treasure it," then came the obligatory speech which by tradition has to be shouted down before the boy reaches the end:

> *Mr. President, Gentlemen, a parent once said to me, Now that you have joined the choir, you will find that your whole life will revolve round Temple. This has been absolutely true. In fact it has been one continual 'Round', not, of course, that you could call it a 'Benighted' existence, because we have been well 'Organised'. Seriously though, if it were to end, for some time or other we have to grow up – it's the only way you can grow! – it would leave an emptiness difficult to fill. Therefore I am more than delighted to be asked here tonight and I look forward to taking an active part in the life of the T.U. O Passi Graviora Dabit Deus Huic Quoque Finem, which being loosely translated is, You have endured worse things, God will grant an end to this. SEDET.*

For Organ Week at the City of London School, recitals had been given by Michael Austin and Harry Gabb and Dr. Ball was the third.

The School Hall was packed, Dr.'s personality pleased the whole audience whether the boys were from Temple or not.

Occasionally a small bang, accompanied by a grin, told us that he had hit the backboard of the smaller organ with his toe, no swell pedal!! There was huge applause.

He walked down the aisle and waved his hands, "Oh no! no! don't clap." He came back for an encore, sat at the organ stool and, before swinging his legs over, said thoughtfully, "Something that lasts three minutes, I know," he flicked a few tabs – the stops – and played his own composition, *Song Tune.* Great applause again!

Gordon Reynolds came to the school to judge the House Music Competition and for Michael's playing he wrote:

An exquisite version of a Brahm's Intermezzo in which full use of the piano was made, I perhaps could have heard a little more of the bass notes. 17 marks out of 20.

He took the Grade VIII exam and passed with merit, then the great event at Temple was the Royal Service for which Dr. had been preparing the gentlemen and boys for a few weeks.

This was a special entry in Michael's diary. Here at last was the special Service, even Canon Milford was excited.

December 21st

Lord Silsoe wants me to press the button to get started. He said the prayer, then in we went. It was pleasant to head the choir with Andrew as we walked in reverse order. Just inside I saw my parents sitting next to the Headmaster.

Mr. Lamb, the Sacristan, swayed very slowly from side to side in front of us, carrying his staff of office. He turned at the altar briskly, by twisting his right foot, paused to regain balance and proceeded again, slowly swaying in a westerly direction. The church was filled with Benchers in evening dress and their ladies in evening dresses.

We reached the Round Church by the great West door and waited, taking up our standing places. At 7.10 pm when everyone was cold from the open door, a policeman leant round the pillar to speak to The Master, "The Queen has been delayed by traffic but she is coming up Middle Temple Lane now."

The excitement and nervousness rose to a pitch, "Her Majesty has arrived, Sir."

The two Hon. Treasurers were presented, the spotlights went on and Mr. Graham, the cleaner, stood to attention. The Queen and Prince Philip entered.

She was wearing a short white fur coat over a long greeny-blue dress. Her diamonds out-dazzled everyone present.

Then we were led down the Church, our backs to the Queen, to our usual end of the stalls. We could not see her, but her presence created an atmosphere right through the church which willed us to do everything right and sing our best.

It did go so well that one almost forgot she was there. Just before my solo, 'O Men from the Fields', I thought – here goes, I hope you remember this – then 'How lovely are thy dwellings fair' by Brahms was almost perfect, exciting and full of atmosphere.

Afterwards Dr. Balls' verdict was 'Jolly good!' he was changing his shoes ready to go to the dinner which the Queen was attending in the Middle Temple Hall. At the next practice Dr. said we had sung the very best since the War. He thought it was marvellous. He repeated that the Queen had said in her speech 'that incomparable choir.'. How thrilling to be Head Boy at a time like this. Dr. gave us the evening off!

Ray's special Christmas present that year was a recording we had made secretly for him at Temple with Dr. at the organ, when Michael sang all his solos, a recording which we still have.

We had imagined that his voice would break soon after but he was to continue singing as Head Boy for two years giving more and more of an alto quality.

He looked forward to his piano lessons with Roy Jesson every fortnight. He took a bus across to Hampstead to Roy's house and had to walk up a steep hill. One day he saw, "parked sideways, because of the hill, a small two wheeled box, resting on poles which extended upwards and turned themselves into handlebars. A man was seated at these pedalling for all he was worth. No one enlightened him that he was going nowhere very fast indeed; I could see sparks flying. But on drawing level I found whirling stone blades and the sharpening of knives." A good description for an English essay that week.

He was studying Schumann's piano concerto with Roy and for his sixteenth birthday we took him to the Festival Hall for a meal and then a concert in which Arrau was playing the concerto.

It was thrilling for all three of us as we were so used to hearing Michael practise it at home. Sir Adrian Boult conducted, it was a splendid performance and Michael remarked that the fairly slow speed had given him the greatest confidence. "I have the right impression that the concerto is a light, romantic and lyrical piece of writing, not a Beethovenistic piece." A few months later he played it with the school orchestra.

That summer Dr. was taken ill and had to have a series of operations. Canon Milford gave Michael the first news when he arrived for the 8.30 Communion Service one Sunday and together with Dr's secretary, Joyce East, and a gentleman of the choir, Donald Lee, they arranged how the service should go, having booked the only organist available at short notice. Michael showed the rather large lady organist the stops and it was very evident that she was "lost". "Are those crescendo pedals?" "Oh, what are those?"

Michael groaned inwardly, luckily Ian le Grice arrived, a former chorister who was learning the organ, and they all decided he should play the service and she, the hymns and voluntaries, but changing the settings to Stanford in B flat and the anthem, *Call to Remembrance*, meant that Michael conducted it partly unaccompanied, so all was well.

Dr.'s stay in hospital lasted a few months so Dr. Harold Darke came to take all the practices and services. His methods were very different. Michael said, "He won't let us have our growing notes, but instead makes us leap for high notes *pp* which is very difficult. I am not allowed to conduct the choir, Dr. Darke does it from the organ and I am sure the tempos are too slow; the rhythm is alive and exact which is very good, and there is zest in it but it is all one lump of overpowering Victoriana. It is terrible to hear and not be able to pull it together."

He went to see Dr. in hospital and they had a good talk, and discussed *Fortifications on how to Sing* – every note a growing note, growing reciting notes, the meaning of words and not the chant, the most important in psalms, change of tempo and lightening in tone at unimportant words or little words so that emphasis is placed on the main meaning of the sentence – for instance, *I am the light of the world, he that followeth me shall not walk in darkness but shall have the light of life* – emphasis on *I am, – light – followeth me – light of life* – in Dr. Ball's words, 'this adds flavour to a dull strictly sung piece of music'.

Michael felt that Dr. Darke had walked in with hobnailed boots and trampled on all Dr.'s carefully built rules for the choir but the weeks soon sped by and Sir William McKie took over the services.

Michael wrote in his diary:

> *Out of the Darke Ages and into the Victory of Sir William over Harold.*
>
> *Sir William went through the music with me, he is going to do everything our way in Temple tradition and is even going to let me conduct. Isn't it wonderful.*
>
> *Sir William said "I want you to think of me as just a substitute for a while, please do it your usual way and I will just accompany you."*
>
> *Marvellous – three cheers for Sir William McKie!*
>
> *I am now sitting my, 'O' levels at school, French, General Classics, English, Latin, Maths, and Science.*

Michael quite liked exams and getting mornings or afternoons off between them.

One day during an exam a sonic boom shook the school hall with such vigour that the black soot cascaded down from the encrusted beams. "At first we thought it was Yogi Bear – Mr. Hargreaves, giving some class a delightful explosive entertainment in the labs!"

At last with additional Maths and Music they were all over. During the summer break Michael travelled to Milborne Port to his Godfather, principally to sing for two services, he wrote:

> *"The organist Sam Burch was very helpful but forgot one or two things in the accompaniments. The inhabitants of the village said it was grand to have me*

there. It is wonderful to stay at the Vicarage. The atmosphere is terrific to be in. I never forget my previous visits, we have family prayers every morning except Sunday. I know that I have a great friend in Uncle Edmund to whom I could always go."

The choir spent several days at Shepperton Studios recording the backing songs for the new film *Oliver* and Michael also recorded the hymn, *Abide With Me* for the Remembrance Service for the Island of Jersey.

There was a nice piece written in the local paper afterwards:

In the presence of His Excellency the Lieut. Governor Vice Admiral Sir Michael Villiers and Lady Villiers, the Jersey Branch of the British Legion staged its Annual Festival of Remembrance at West Park Pavilion. After the tribute came the Muster and the Queen's message was read by Lt. Col. P.A.O. Northey. The Band of the Island played a selection of French melodies. As usual, part three of the Festival, The Remembrance, was poignant and a feature was a beautiful recording of "Abide With Me" by Master Michael James, head chorister of the Temple Church, London, specially recorded, unaccompanied, at the Temple Church. In his address, the Dean of Jersey, the Very Revd. A. S. Giles said, "Remembrance is not an act of sentimentality, nor is it an attempt to glorify war. It is an expression of an essential part of every man's life. That is the ability to remember – to remember to plan our lives so that we can avoid those things that are unworthy and find those things that are true and just. There is not glory in war, but there is glory in those who make sacrifice in war."

There was more and more pressure in his school work and the disappointing, but quite extraordinary, news that he had failed Music 'O' level. No one understood why, but he was told to plough on and take Music at 'A' level instead.

He completed writing a flute Sonata and a set of songs and he had sketched in an idea for an anthem *Twas in the Cool of Eventide*.

Dr. Ball finally came back to Temple and he and Michael talked at depth about the choir and of all that had happened during the 'Interregnum' – Dr. said "Do you know Michael, Harold came to me at the Clinic and actually had the effrontery to say he was getting the tone better and it would soon be like 'Kings' (Kings College, Cambridge, with which there was great rivalry at the time). In the explosion which followed evidently Dr. Ball said, "Heaven Forbid." The two buildings were so entirely different and the 'tones' were designed for the buildings themselves.

Finally came the last week of Michael's life at Temple, eight years was a very long time to have been a chorister and two and a half years of those as Head Boy, he wrote:

> *It was a hard and exhausting time during Dr Ball's absence but we all pulled through and the choir has not lost any of its standards. Now he is back, these last months have been perfect, we were all so overjoyed that the atmosphere has been very good.*
>
> *I think there are more day dreamers now than there were a few years ago, there does not seem to be the total dedication in all the boys, but the probationers have come out of their shells, most promising and Kim especially so. Oh, what a lesson to be learned. In the anthem he*

sits engrossed in the copy, mouthing the words and each note, looking up and following my lead and changes of tempo – all from the probationers seats. He will be Head Boy one day, I'm sure.

The funniest thing happened on my way down from the organ loft the other day – Derek and Andrew tried to de-bag me. Nigel was also there but just giggled all the time and Andrew felt it beneath him to help. However, I did not resist which took the wind out of their sails. I then went up to the Master's house in a cassock to hide and think, and the Master, twinkling with his merry internal laughter, lent me a pair of trousers to surprise the boys.

This is where the Whitehall farce begins! Coming down the stairs in my six feet long, rolled up at the turn-ups, baggy trousers, I met the Dean of Worcester, who is to be the new Master of the Temple.

He said, " You wouldn't happen to be the Head Boy, would you?"

"Yes sir, I am, how do you do. Unfortunately I shall not be here when you begin your term of office."

"Isn't it always the way," Dean Milburn replied. "Well, I hope you have a good worthy chap to follow you, who will carry on with quietness and good sense."

Canon Milford and I exchanged a look, thinking of the ironic subplot which at the time was proceeding downstairs!

In the end he collected my trousers and I was able to go home without the encumbrance of the farcical ones.

July 28th. The last Sunday. The Introit was, *The Lord God Omnipotent reigneth. Let us rejoice and be glad and give honour unto Him.* Psalms 128, 129, 130 and 131. Te Deum, Alcock in B flat, Jubilate Deo, Stanford in B flat and the Anthem, Laudamus te, J.S.Bach. The *Tarry no Longer* was especially poignant for us today:

Tarry no longer, towards thine heritage
Haste on thy way and be of right good cheer.
Go each day onward on thy pilgrimage.
Think how short time thou shalt abide thee here.
Thy place is built above the starris clear!
None earthly palace, wrought in so stately wise.
Come on my friend, my brother most dear!
For thee I offered my blood in sacrifice.
Tarry no longer!

John Lydgate

Dr. Ball's voluntary was the Fugue in E flat, St. Anne. J.S.Bach.

Michael wrote:

Back in the practice room the gentlemen presented me with two volumes of Bach's organ music with this inscription on a card:-

To Michael

In appreciation of a long and well played innings as head boy of the Temple Church Choir. From the gentlemen of the choir.

July 1968

Dr. Ball gave me a copy, signed, of his hymn variations and Mummy and Daddy gave me a new watch with the message, 'For this special day to remember, psalm 129, verse 8, part 2'. I didn't need to look it up, for we had just sung it that morning – 'The Lord prosper you, We wish you good luck in the Name of the Lord'.

~·~·~·~·~·~·~·~

Durham University

S ometimes I listen to music and am analysing it so that I can hear a cadence or phrase and consider why the composer put it in just that place, showing he was a genius, otherwise he wouldn't have done so. But sometimes I just listen and it seems to touch thoughts and feelings deep down inside me that I hardly knew existed. There's a depth in me that only music can touch, that is why I must make music my life's work.

A solemn moment in the summertime of 1968. He was preparing for Music, History and English 'A' levels, he was already considering to which Universities he would apply, but also saying that a year in between school and University would be good, to attend the Royal College of Music.

That summer he joined the British Youth Wind Orchestra in a residential course in Birmingham and they gave the final concert in Coventry Cathedral.

The Wind Orchestra had been established as the splendid offshoot of the British Youth Symphony Orchestra which Michael had joined the previous holiday.

Having played the timpani in the City of London School Orchestra, he was accepted into the percussion group and alongside him then, was a much younger boy, Simon Rattle!!

Michael played the timps with great gusto and skill; he particularly enjoyed Zadok the Priest and the first performance in this country of Herbert Haufrecht's Symphony for brass and timpani.

The concert in Coventry Cathedral ended with the performance of Grand Symphonie Funebre et Triomphale by Hector Berlioz, conducted by Bryan Fairfax.

But there were two fine concerts in Birmingham and London with the British Youth Symphony Orchestra, one in Birmingham and the other at the Festival Hall in London.

At the Festival Hall Michael was one of a hundred or so musicians between the ages of eighteen and twenty-two. He found it very thrilling to be playing in the Festival Hall for the first time and with such a distinguished conductor as Sir Adrian Boult. The most exciting performance of the whole programme was the Brahms Second Symphony.

In the autumn we wrote to the Temple Choir Committee:

We would like to personally thank you for all you have done for our son Michael during the time that he has been a member of the choir. Dr. Ball enrolled him as a probationer in the autumn of 1960 and he has now left - an 'old man' of 17, after two and a half years as head boy.

It is not only difficult to speak of the full value of these eight years at Temple for a boy who is going to make a career of music; he will be realising this throughout his life; but it is also difficult to express adequately the gratitude we feel for your support and encouragement in maintaining his education at the City of London School, an education which, combined with the environment of the Temple, must be one of the finest in the country.

We know that the dedication of the choir and the beauty of the music for the Services must repay you in part, but we hope you will accept our sincere wishes and thanks for giving Michael such a golden opportunity to share in them.

Someone said to us in 1960 that our lives would begin to revolve around the Temple Church. This happened, and went on happening and long may it continue to happen.

Our very good wishes to you all,

    Sincerely,

        Margaret and Raymond James

Our reply came soon after:

Parliament Chamber
Inner Temple, London EC4
16th October 1968
Dear Mr. and Mrs. James,

As Chairman of the Choir Committee I brought before the Choir Committee yesterday afternoon your letter of the 3rd October. The Choir Committee were most appreciative of your letter and asked me to write and thank you very cordially for writing to them as you have. It really is to all of us on the Committee a source of intense gratification to hear from you and to read your most generously and kindly worded letter.

We have been, all of us, most fortunate in having your son with us as a member of the Temple Choir. Everybody must be extremely proud of the choir and we all owe a debt of gratitude to the choir boys and choir men who sing in it and also to Dr. Thalben-Ball for his work in connection with the training of the choir. It was particularly agreeable to read in your letter of your thought with regard to the connection that we all of us have with the Temple and we each of us agree with you that such a connection is something of infinite value which goes with us for the whole of our lives.

May I, on behalf of the Choir Committee, take this opportunity of sending our very best wishes both to Michael and to you and once again thank you most cordially for writing as you have.

Yours sincerely,
Stow Hill.

Dr. Ball had said once, and it was quoted in David Lewer's book about Temple, *A Spiritual Song*, "We whose natures and minds have been moulded by the Temple, are the guardians of a very precious thing, a thing not made with hands and which cannot be gotten for gold."

Our home, in Dorset Street, off Baker Street, was still our much loved base, although the traffic was getting more and more dense. It was a wonderfully convenient place to be for anything or any place we needed.

Michael described the atmosphere in this way:

To say that London wakes up, is not a true statement of the facts, for London is awake all the time.

There are the night trains, there is the hurried bustle of the sorting offices channelling the mail to all various districts by private underground.

There are the Night Security Patrols, the steady paces of policemen's feet, the jangling sirens and bells as the night-shift firemen, blue lights whirling, clatter down the empty streets.

The traffic lights continue to change incessantly and the shops still exhibit their goods in full lighting in the hope that no intruders will break in, so nothing is dark. But if someone is tempted, a high pitched persistent bell will jingle until daybreak in somebody's dreams.

Charladies scrub on soft kneeling pads and slop and hoover, flashing the lights from room to room and floor to floor which makes the high rise buildings look like busy computers.

The first bus down Baker Street changes gear and roars

away, the early milk float whines its electric motor and stops with a resounding click. The metallic noise of milk bottle meeting doorstep passes up the street and a dog barks.

The birds flap-flap away and after circling, land with a complacent shrug and tuck their wings away.

Traffic can be heard to rumble down the main road in ever-increasing waves; a lorry growls up the mews and slamming of doors and men's deep voices tell me that the workmen are here to dig up the cobbled surface.

Short bells ring as shops are unlocked and burglar alarms turned off. Trudging feet of the commuters tell of a surge from Baker Street Station; all is now rumbling, grumbling noise.

The traffic, the door slamming, dog barking, street calling day has begun.

We had been in a smokeless zone for some years and it was extraordinary how clean the air smelt, either first thing in the morning or late at night. In the Spring, blossoms in Regents Park wafted scent right down Baker Street if the wind was from the north, and we could always tell when the lilac was out even if we hadn't been walking in the park for a week or two.

Michael was now in his last year at school, which was taken up entirely with work for his three 'A' levels: music, history and English. They were three difficult subjects to have chosen to do together, for all of them required at least two essays a week. His colleagues who had Maths as well as English were considered, 'having an easy time', though I'm sure they were not.

Michael was definite about having a year at the Royal College of Music so that was settled, and then came the pouring over reams of details about the various Universities to which to apply. As a first suggestion the school advised trying for a choral scholarship, so with an application to Cambridge went the two required letters of recommendation, one from Dr. Ball and the other from Roy Jesson.

The Temple, London.

I have known Michael James for a number of years. He was leader of choristers of the Temple Church during which time I became very aware of his great interest in music. I have formed an opinion that he is unusually gifted in musical sense and ability. I am delighted to support his application for a choral award.

George Thalben-Ball

Hampstead, N.W.3.

I am very glad to write in support of Michael James's application for admission to the college. Michael has studied piano privately with me for the past four years. He has exceptional musical talent and high intelligence and has made excellent progress. Evidence of his musicianship and technical control was his recent performance of the 1st Movement of Schumann's Piano Concerto with his school orchestra, which was of a very high standard and showed a mature and sensitive understanding of the music, as well as poise and confidence. I am sure he will make the best use of any help that can be afforded to him.

Roy Jesson, M.A., B.Mus., Ph.D. Professor, R.A.M.

Accordingly Michael went to Cambridge, but his application was turned down and we were really not surprised for his adult singing voice was in no way settled. In fact, it was to be several years before his rich baritone was in evidence.

The 'A' levels were taken and he left the City of London School on July 16th 1969. The long wait for results was rewarded in August with the news of all three passed with Grades B & C and with this news came the letters to say he was expected to attend at four Universities, Exeter, Surrey, Durham and York for consideration of his applications.

Exeter he quite liked, mostly for the fact of the Cathedral close by. Surrey was in a very new state, the music department only just opening, but Guildford Cathedral was only a few steps away. York music department was good but a long way from the Cathedral and the University seemed to Michael to have a very secular atmosphere, but Durham – and then one has to stop to draw breath – his own words!

Durham, its Castle and Cathedral high on the great promontory above the town and he had an interview where his character and personality were considered as essential as the music. The great music library and the whole atmosphere of the music department was a perfect place in which to spend three years.

He arrived back home having thoroughly enjoyed it all, including the railway journeys, of course. There arrived on the mat several days later, three large envelopes. He had been offered places at Durham, York and Surrey. Without hesitation he accepted Durham and would start there in October 1970.

Meanwhile there was a happy year at the R.C.M. His tutors

were Richard Latham, Richard Popplewell and Herbert Howells and it was with Dr. Howells that he became particularly close in friendship. The great composer had lost his son Michael some years before; he took our Michael into his warmth and guidance and as he said to me once, "We are studying composition together!"

Michael did, indeed, study composition with Herbert Howells; on one occasion they sat together in Hereford Cathedral listening to a performance of his great choral work, *Hymnus Paradisi.*

Howells', at Michael's age, had sat with Elgar at a performance of *The Dream of Gerontius.* He turned to Michael saying that they were making it sound better than he had thought and then, "Oh dear, I don't like that", or "Not bad, eh!" Michael invited him to attend the Temple Union Dinner one year as his guest and he remarked that there he was, sitting with the two great Doctors, one on each side; he was so proud to be with them.

There was also the choir at the Royal College of Music in which Michael took part in the splendid performance of Vaughan Williams Sea Symphony. A review of the performance was very favourable complimenting the College, Choir, and orchestra on their 'well-knit performance' and 'coping to the full with Whitman's salty and bracing verses'. John Russell, the conductor, gained praise for his firm control and 'securing good ensembles in the big choral passages'. The baritone, Timothy Rowe, was reported to have 'shown real feeling for the words and music as he was no doubt aware that the director of the College, Sir Keith Faulkner, present in the audience, had himself sung the work with Vaughan Williams'.

During that year at College he played the organ in the little chapel of St. George's Hospital, Hyde Park, for Sunday services and also worked at the Wigmore Hall on many occasions as stage director. It was his responsibility to make sure that the musicians' stands and chairs were placed correctly and to judge by the audience applause, when an artist should return to the stage and perhaps play an encore. It was a wonderful opportunity to listen to a wide range of music and to absorb some of the good and interesting performances the different artists gave.

He was to be very thankful for that year before going to Durham. It widened his horizons and experience and he was to realize the difference it had made to him, when comparing himself to young men just arriving at Durham straight from school. They took much longer to settle to the new atmosphere and even longer to stand on their own feet, away from home for the first time.

Durham is the most wonderful place in which to spread ones wings, and just to stand beside the River Wear and gaze at one of the finest sights in Great Britain would be to me, somehow, sufficient. High on the dark red sandstone hill stands Durham Castle. Behind the battlemented walls which are built sheer on the cliffs' edge, are the mellowed smaller houses of the University and beyond, rise the lovely red brown towers of Durham Cathedral.

What a perfect site for a castle and cathedral. The Castle sits on the hill and gathers the little town around it, a tight mass of houses and little winding streets like lanes, leading to the bridges over the river with its rush of water at the weir.

The Castle is now University College; the other colleges are gathered around the central green square on the top of the hill and at the further end of this plateau is the Cathedral. There is a great door in the north porch with a most fascinating and grotesque knocker that has history and legend. When the sound of that knocker reverberated through the church, two monks who were always on duty waiting for such a call, ran down to admit whoever had knocked and take him into Sanctuary. No matter what he had done, he would be safe and one presumes no more harm would come to him.

The Cathedral is magnificent, the greatest perhaps of all Norman churches; it has giant-sized columns, an awe-inspiring roof and arches; the vastness is somehow northern; a graceful pretty church would have been out of place and this stupendous building is there to withstand the weathers and the cragginess of its position, proclaiming its everlasting faith in a changing world.

On our first visit there, Michael met us at the station, hopping up and down with excitement and running along the platform as he saw us, with our heads out of the window, where we had been since the train crawled slowly over the high viaduct and we had caught our first glimpse of the magic hill.

Standing on the green by the Cathedral, a mist swirled about the towers, it seemed to be a timeless scene made even more so when suddenly, a brown robed monk appeared from nowhere and walked gently past us and off into the mist again. We would not have been surprised at anything at that moment for the sense of unreality was very great.

Michael had a room in one of the newer buildings of residence on Palace Green, but later, when he became the organ scholar, he had two fine rooms in the castle itself, the windows overlooking the courtyard and gatehouse, the Keep rising one side and the towers of the Cathedral beyond the gateway.

The world nowadays appears to be in constant change and it is difficult sometimes to stand against the tide of ensuing chaos and doubt. Yet the calmness of worship, inspired perhaps by the uplifting experience of such a view as that hilltop scene, lies deep within me, a well of peace on which to keep hold.

The Tunstal Chapel in the Castle named after Bishop Tunstal who built it about 1542 was Michael's particular place of worship, for it was there as organ scholar that he was in charge of music for the services.

He trained the choir made up of men and women in the college; rehearsal 5-6 pm, service 6-6.40 pm – in Dr. Richard Hall's words, "A short rehearsal time carried out with quiet efficiency and no flap and in freezing weather, keeping up everyone's spirits !" He played the 'Father' Smith organ, the famous organ builder had originally installed in the Cathedral.

The cornice of the organ gallery once formed part of the Cathedral pulpit. But perhaps the most mysteriously beautiful part of the Castle was the Norman Chapel in the Crypt. Carved in soft creamy sandstone, small and intimate, with candles, one cross and a soft whispering of the sand, gently falling from the stones at one's touch. It was there that Michael reintroduced the habit of singing Compline at the end of the day in plainsong chant. There, was the calmness and peace of worship and the sense of God's time, though I read somewhere and it has stayed in my mind – *With God there is no time – only a timeless joy of an eternal present*. One could feel eternity in that chapel.

The whole Castle is full of history dating from about 1,000 A.D. and over the years altered, added to and enriched by the various Bishops whose residence it was.

The University was founded in 1832 but as early as the time of King Henry VIII the idea had been discussed to have a northern University, and from 1836 the Castle has been used for the purposes of the University and is occupied by the staff and students of University College.

The great dining hall has a fine and beautiful timber roof, very like the Middle Temple Hall, filled with refectory tables and long benches where the students have their main meals with waitresses to serve them; the head table was at the end of the Hall, where the Master of the College and staff dined and the dais where Latin grace was said on high days and holidays.

There is a vast black oak staircase and a gallery and the Keep and the Bishop's rooms and also rooms in which the Judges of the Assize still stay.

When we attended the Congregation in which the degrees were given, our bedroom in the Castle had a large skylight and during a heavy rainstorm this leaked and our bed was soaked through.

Michael went to see the porter and the only other bed available was the large four-poster in the Bishop's Room. We were accordingly allowed to occupy the Bishop's suite of rooms and they were absolutely marvellous.

The walls were covered in the most magnificent tapestries and paintings – Rembrandt, Van Dyck and the like – and the bed was huge and luxuriously counterpaned. The bathroom had the biggest bath we had ever seen, it was of Victorian splendour, and the toilet had a mahogany surround with a decorated porcelain chain pull. The carpets were so thick that our feet sank into them and all the windows were curtained in rich brocades and silks. We could see right across the city from the windows, deeply set into the thick walls; we were high above the surrounding countryside.

Michael conducted DULOG, the Durham Light Opera Company, in the first year, *The Gondoliers* by Gilbert and Sullivan and *Fra Diavalo* during the second year.

One of the glories of the summer term was to sit on the banks of the river and listen to the singing of madrigals from the boats as they lazily floated by. At midnight there was still light in the sky so far north.

One summer day he had been sitting on the river bank working and studying and a swan came out of the water and walked up to him. He wrote:

I felt very vulnerable six inches from an inquisitive pecking beak. It tried to eat some of my orchestration horn parts (best place for them).

There were the Balls and parties and June week with dancing and concerts and festivals; it was during Michael's first June week that I saw him conduct the Gondoliers. The Castle Choir visited Durham Prison and sang in various local churches and often broadcast on local Radio Durham.

Then there is the Kiosk Tea and Coffee Shop menu-card with such delicacies as celery hearts wrapped in ham and grilled with cheese – by this time the prices have become 'decimal' and if one had celery hearts with new potatoes it would cost 40 pence. Poached egg on toast 15 pence. Grilled, on request – mushrooms on toast 17½ pence. The prices are unbelievable – Teas per pot per person 9 pence – Coffee 7½ pence. How inflation rocketed after that!

In 1970-1973 estimates of annual fees and expenses were:

Maintenance Fee - board and residence	*£214.10.0*
Tuition Fees for candidates in the Faculty of Arts	*£58.10.0*
Other Annual expenses - approx.	
Buttery and Bar Account and Teas	*£35.0.0*
Books and Stationery, etc.	*£35.0.0*
Voluntary subscriptions	*£5.0.0*
Matriculation & Registration Fee	*£3.0.0*
Caution Money (returnable)	*£10.0.0*
Gown - on entry - new	*£5.0.0*
- second-hand	*£1.0.0*

The Durham Union Society had a series of debates each year. For instance:

This House would like to see the election of a Liberal Party Government and the speaker for the proposition was David Steel, Esq. M.P. for Roxburgh, Selkirk and Peebles.

This House wishes that Guy Fawkes had succeeded. For the proposition Wilfred Bramble, Esq. Star of stage, screen and television – Steptoe's father.

This House believes that Freedom of Speech should be limited to those who do not abuse it. For the proposition Bernard Levin, Esq. Daily Mail columnist and broadcaster, for the opposition Paul Foot, Esq. Militant member of the New Left.

This House believes that the moral code of the individual should not be determined by the Church. For the proposition, Rt. Rev. The Lord Bishop of Durham, for the opposition, The Earl of Longford.

This House believes that the artist is essentially a decorator. For the proposition, Dr. Fitzpatrick, Lecturer in Philosophy at the University, for the opposition, Hugh McDairmid, Esq., Scotland's National Poet.

Castle Day was May 15th in 1971. After lunch in the Great Hall when the Castle Minstrels sang, there was coffee and drinks in the Undercroft. Evensong in Tunstal Chapel, Tea in the Courtyard, *Diversions* in the Fellows' Garden and then the Castle Ball with four different bands. Floreat Castellum at 1.00 a.m. Carriages at 1.30. Cloaks may be left at the entrance to the Black Staircase. Dress formal.

A Night of Revelry on the Ocean Bed to be held at 60 fathoms in the Great Hall (by kind permission of Poseidon). Diving will commence at 8.30, Decompression 2 a.m. In between there were Sub-Aquatic Entertainments. Plankton will be served in Davey Jones's Locker and one could drown one's sorrows in the Norman or Minstrel Gallery. The Candlemas Ball did not finish until 4 a.m. when breakfast was served.

Apart from actually being at University to read one's subject, what a wonderfully fulfilling three years, literally a time to get to know oneself and to blossom and flourish.

Conrad Eden, the organist of the Cathedral, was giving Michael lessons and during the holidays he was still the organist at St. George's Hospital, Hyde Park Corner, London and for that he was given the princely sum of £60 per year. There is a list of organ voluntaries dated March – April, 1972 which were obviously in his repertoire by then:

Sunday, 19 March	*Chorale-Prelude Herzlich that mich verlasgen – J.S.Bach*
Sunday, 26 March	*Fantasia in G.min. BWV 542 – J.S.Bach*
Friday, 31 March	*Good Friday. Chorale-Prelude Passion Chorale – J.S.Bach*
Sunday, 2 April	*Easter Sunday. Chorale-Prelude Nun Danket Alle Gott – Karg Elert*
Sunday, 9 April	*Low Sunday Organ Voluntary in D – J. Stanley*
Sunday, 16 April	*Easter 2. Chorale-Prelude "HYFRODOL" – G.T.Ball*

Sunday, 23 April   *St. George's Day. Cromhorne sure la Jaille – Couperin*
       6.30   *Hospital Evensong - Great Fantasia & Fugue in G Minor*
    – J.S.Bach

During this time we moved from Dorset Street right out into the country in Kent. The traffic and noise had become unbearable since Baker Street had been made into a one-way system and we thought if we were deep in the country it would be wonderful, but, in fact, it was a disaster. Ray was travelling for hours, we hardly saw each other, and disheartened, we looked for somewhere to live nearer London.

We found a dear little modern house – a box, all windows, but nevertheless quite ideal at the time, in Forest Hill near Dulwich. It had a walled garden at the rear and in the front there was a long garden filled with trees and lilies of the valley in May, looking onto a leafy quiet road.

Opposite the house stood the tall spired parish church in its churchyard garden, and from our front kitchen window I could watch the weddings and Christenings and funerals, or just enjoy the quiet peace of a building for worship with the birds lazily circling the spire.

It was a dear little house and we were very happy there; guessing that we might be there only a few years, for a little later on we should probably have to find a larger house so that my Mother could come and live with us, we called our Forest Hill house, *Stepping Stones*.

We never felt cold there for the sun came in every available window and the back of the house was a veritable suntrap. In fact, we had slatted blinds at the windows in the height of summer to cut the glare. After a while we longed for somewhere a little shadier, but that was in rare moments.

In 1973 Michael brought the choir from Durham to sing the services in Southwark Cathedral for a week. They all camped in the hall of the church opposite and came over to us for baths and talks and special meals. That week at Southwark was to have far-reaching effects.

When Michael was home during the holidays he cycled round and about Forest Hill. The roads were wide and leafy and it was pleasantly quiet in the back streets. He discovered a small modern church one day and stopped to read the notice board, the church was dedicated to Dietrich Bonnhoffer. He wondered what kind of organ it had and if he might practice there some day; at any rate it was interesting to find a German church.

Subsequently passing it again one day he noticed a man out in the garden emptying a teapot into a flower bed and supposing him to be the carctaker, he wheeled his bicycle up the drive and spoke to him asking if it was at all possible to try the organ there.

The man looked at him incredulously. "Are you an organist?" he asked, "I've been praying for an organist! Come in! Come in!"

He was Pastor Honnegger who had been praying all morning, for he didn't know how he would get through the following Sunday services without music. Michael spoke a little German which he learned during the first year at Durham as it was so useful for studying Lieder, so the two spoke haltingly together in the two languages.

He was hurried to the console and only played a few notes before the Pastor was smiling and clasping him by the hand.

Michael played there many times. It was fascinating to have the whole service in German. He had to have special cues to enable him to know the exact moment to play, for the service was slightly different from the usual Anglican Matins or Eucharist.

One morning I accompanied him for one of his practices. Sitting just below the long modern stained glass windows in the beautiful small church and hearing Michael playing Bach, I lost the deep sense of fear and hatred, if that is not too strong a description, that I had felt since the war. The bombing we had gone through, the death and destruction, the discovery of the concentration camps – it had left such deep impressions and, after all, had happened barely thirty years before. The feeling of peace was overwhelming, it made me realise the healing power at work in all the seemingly little events, the coincidences of chance meetings, perhaps not just coincidences after all, but a sure pattern we could follow if we were in tune with God day by day.

The three years of Durham were speeding by and all too soon came the extensive preparations for the exams.

Ray sent Michael the Temple Service sheet one month with the observation that there was an innovation at Morning Service:

> *A threefold Amen after the blessing which took everyone in the congregation by surprise. I approve of course, it is the finishing touch that rounds off the Service. In case you are looking for a vehicle for a musical composition for a thesis, the sermon given by the Master might serve the purpose. He quoted Marco Polo's version of his understanding of the Three Wise Men – the Magi –*

certainly astrologers, but wise – I don't know.

Briefly the idea was that the youngest "King", about 20 years old went in to meet the Christ child and present his gift. The child surprised him by being about his own age. The second King aged about 40 years also went in and was disturbed to find him aged 40. When the third King came out he told them that the child was his age, a very old man.

After some deliberation they decided to go in together – great thinking for wise men! and were astounded to find a baby.

Can you imagine Britten or Menotti dealing with that?

Much love as ever, hope you are settling in well and able to do the listening you needed.

Regards to Jane, all the prettiest girls come from Dorset tell her – Your Dad.

Soon after this, however, it was Chloe who was the companion, sweet and lovely, large dark eyes with a charming and dreamy personality, her one drawback seemingly was that she didn't like opera!

She and Michael were a great help to each other during the strain of heavy study and were finally both successful in their different degrees, hers in philosophy and Michael's in music, a 2/1 honours B.A. So there we were back in Durham for the ceremony and we stayed overnight in the Bishop's Rooms.

Congregation Day – Friday, July 6th 1973 and on July 7th a service was held for the University of Durham in the Cathedral, with the sermon given by the Reverend J.C.P. Cockerton, the Principal of St. John's College.

The hymns were chosen because they were inspired from psalms. *God of Mercy, God of Grace* – Psalm 67; *Praise the Lord, ye heavens adore him* – Psalm 148 and the Anthem with words from Psalm 81 and music by William Crotch *Sing we merrily unto God our strength – make a cheerful noise unto the God of Jacob.* The cheerful noise of the packed congregation in the Cathedral was overwhelming, so many young voices enthusiastically lifting the roof, a wonderful overture to the splendid and magnificent dignity of the whole celebration.

The degree ceremony was held in the Great Hall of the Castle –the Academic Procession entered headed by the Mace of the University, carried by the Beadle. It consisted of members of the Academic Staff in gowns and hoods and full academic dress, the Governing Bodies of the University and the Chancellor at the rear. The congregation remained standing until the Chancellor declared the Congregation open. The degrees were then awarded.

The Honorary Degrees were conferred first. The Registrar of the University rose and announced that the Dean of the Faculty 'prays leave' to present candidates qualified to receive degrees. The Chancellor called upon the Dean formally to present the candidates, he then read out the name of each candidate led forward in alphabetical order by the Beadle.

A very long line of graduates moved forward amid a lot of applause – "By the authority of the University I admit this candidate to the degree of B.A. Honours" – the black hood edged with white fur is placed round the neck and the Chancellor shakes hands – we were proud enough and so keyed up with it all we hardly knew whether to smile or cry, I think we did both.

Outside in the Castle courtyard the Master of University College, said that we were to be congratulated on our son, "Michael has given us much more in these three years than we have given him, it has been a privilege to have him here".

We all stood around on Palace Green in the bright sunshine, the glorious colours of the academic gowns and Elizabethan headgear contrasting with the black gowns of the Graduates and their hoods and mortar boards, the ladies in summer dress and hats and the wonderful feeling of things well done and all right with the world.

Michael came down from Durham with his trunk and cases bulging with music and books, posters and papers and all the paraphernalia collected during three years of a busy life.

From this period he hardly ever threw anything away, but I am very grateful to him for being able to sift through so much material to help me write this account. He had been guided to take and had decided upon a further year of study for a Certificate of Education to enable him to teach and accordingly, he was accepted at Jesus College, Cambridge for the next academic year.

He was asked to do two weeks teaching in September as a preliminary exercise. The small Church of England Junior School just down the road at Forest Hill was chosen and he spent two weeks in the happy midst of South London infants, thoroughly enjoying himself. He found it a challenge.

It was the beginning of the open plan classes, children deciding on their subjects. In guidance and conversation, the lessons would evolve in any direction, to the delight and surprise of all concerned. I think he was very lucky to have been allocated a school where all the children came from similar backgrounds, with parents eager to encourage the whole educational system, so the children were eager to learn and discipline was maintained. At any rate he was not discouraged by the experience and regaled us many times with the humorous and delightful stories of what had occurred during the day.

The transition from Durham to Cambridge could not have been easier and to be a Graduate at Jesus College had a sense of position without the pressure that is asserted on an Undergraduate. It was also enhanced by the position of Assistant Organist at Jesus College Chapel.

Walking around Cambridge one day I said, "How do you manage to find yourself in such wonderful places?" I was really making a statement, not asking a question; the Temple, Durham and Cambridge were three soul-filling environments, to walk along the Backs and explore the Cambridge Colleges, ones spirit could only rise.

Michael cycled like everyone else, a registered number painted in large figures on the mudguard of the bicycle. It was never padlocked, but if it disappeared it could be traced to the other side of the town at another college entrance or gateway where some one had borrowed it in a great hurry and left it to be collected, with a note of apology. Does that happen now I wonder?

Just after the New Year of 1974 Michael passed the A.R.C.O. exam and became an Associate of the Royal College of Organists. He had tried twice before and failed. He said he could never spare the time to concentrate on just that set of exams, both written and practical as there was always so much else to do. However, now he had passed it and we attended the Diploma Presentation at the R.C.O. on January 20th.

That first term at Jesus College had evidently been very rewarding, studying psychology and teaching in general, as well as all aspects of teaching music; the next term was to be the Practical one and he was sent to Guildford Grammar School.

A governor of the school was to tell us some years later, that Michael had made his personality felt there in just that one term and had been remembered long after. The summer term he was back at Jesus College and had his first organ lesson with Gillian Weir, the famous organ recitalist, on the organ of Clare College, and over the next few years he occasionally travelled back to Cambridge for a lesson with her. He said she was exciting and great fun to be with; on two occasions she asked him to turn pages for her at a recital. She would be wearing a fabulous gown with interesting detail on the back, the most seen by the audience, the skirt reaching the ground and draping gracefully over the organ stool but at the console side, the skirt pulled up to the knees to be out of the way of her fast moving legs and feet on the pedals.

During the last term he made several applications for posts as music teacher and attended interviews, two in Dorset, one for Milton Abbey and one for Canford School near Wimborne.

He not only greatly liked Canford, the Christian based teaching and environment, but realised how wonderful it would be to work in Dorset. Visiting the coast there for camp as a boy every year, he had come to love it; the deep countryside, the many varied types of landscape so near. It was obvious if he was lucky enough to be given the post at Canford, he would need a car and would have to learn to drive.

A letter arrived offering him the post of Assistant Director of Music from the Headmaster of Canford School. He joyfully accepted and at the same time gained his Certificate of Education with two distinctions from Jesus College.

Then came one of those kindly acts for which one can ever be grateful and which was one of the beautifully coloured threads in the making and weaving of Michael's life: he was given a small car, as a gift, in perfect working order. A 1963 Wolsley 1300, four doors, real leather seats, wooden dashboard and only 2,000 miles on the clock. His benefactor, Miss Pat Patterson – our good friend – decided that keeping her little car in a garage in Chelsea was not the right thing to do as she only used it occasionally, perhaps once a month at the most, Michael would be the best person to look after it, and make the most use of it.

She had known us since her frequent visits to the Temple Church when Michael was a chorister. He went to her flat with a friend who could drive and brought the car to Forest Hill. He had three lessons at the local driving school and passed the driving test first time.

We all laughed together at the thought of that little blue car years ago in Regents Park which he drove like a veteran at the age of four, perhaps he really had learned to drive then – at any rate, he practised his driving down all the quiet roads around Forest Hill and Sydenham, through Penge and Crystal Palace and gradually ventured further and further afield, Sidney, for so he called his car, was to stand him in good stead until 1980 when he had the chance of buying a second-hand Ford Cortina, but Sidney had travelled many a thousand miles, up to Scotland, to Wales, and regularly back and forth from Dorset to London along the motorways.

Canford School, Wimborne

Visiting Michael at his home, The Elms, shared with two other bachelor teachers, was always a happy experience.

The Elms was the middle cottage of a short row of three in the grounds of the school looking out onto a little stream, a fir tree and a grassy walk. He had his own study/sitting room and bedroom and shared the kitchen and bathroom. I helped him by making the curtains, he chose the material at the local shop in Wimborne.

The first thing of value he bought for himself, when he was earning a very good salary for the first time, was a grandfather clock. It dates from 1830, has a steady tick – nice and slow and a melodious hourly chime. But it has to be stopped at bedtime, as tuneful though it is, the chime is penetrating. When he was fourteen he suddenly announced that when he got married we could buy him a grandfather clock, but as an afterthought "Mind you – a double bed would be more useful".

A second-hand upright piano with candelabrum was the next acquisition, quite good enough for practising and setting work for the boys. He loved being a schoolmaster, and that first term the post of assistant organist at Wimborne Minster became vacant, he applied and was accepted. This made his life complete. Barry Ferguson was the organist and choir master of the Minster at that time.

The car sped from Canford to Wimborne and back several times a day and when he became conductor of the Blandford Choral Society he travelled there once a week.

Sherborne had a marvellous music shop, which meant a good journey through the deep Dorset countryside, and visits to Salisbury were a delight, also to Winchester for an occasional lesson with James Lancelot at the Cathedral.

Michael seemed to work forty-eight hours in every twenty-four and visits to him, lasting two days perhaps, would feel like a whole week of activity. We drove further afield to the great prehistoric sites of Dorset, the standing stones and the Cerne Abbas giant and the huge dragon hill, Bulbarrow. Dorset had a primeval air; one could feel the presence of thousands of years of our forebears and the deep reassurance of our history.

The Headmaster at Canford retired and the new Headmaster arrived in 1976. Martin Marriott and his wife, Judith, were to become very good friends. Michael found great difficulty coping with a personality clash in the Masters' common room, it was partly his own fault, trying to do too much, and the artist in him at odds with the teacher, but nevertheless it was a time of unhappiness. It was Martin Marriott who would smooth the paths, and the kitchen in the Headmaster's house became the focal point for love and friendship at Canford with Judith always ready to talk and provide coffee and tea.

Also at this time Barry Ferguson moved on to become organist and Master of the choristers at Rochester Cathedral. He and Michael had worked well together in the Minster; he trained the choir to a high standard and was always striving for perfection. He inspired greater musical effort; in a letter Michael wrote to us about the worship in the Minster:

I am filled with an excitement, perhaps if you like, fired with enthusiasm to master the instrument and the music written for it. I find elements of the Holy Spirit so clearly suggested in Bach's great music, true worship. To me there is no greater act of worship than to develop my gifts in playing this sort of music at a church service.

A young teacher in the Art Department at Canford, Casandra Ward, was an American girl from Arkansas, here for a short while to work and to be a missionary for the World Youth Service. She was three years older than Michael, she was beautiful, he said, "She taught me to pray." They fell in love. He told me once that she was far too good for him and that he could never hope to match the depth of her faith. "You should have seen her when we were in Wales," he said. "She was standing on the top of the mountain, her arms wide, praying into the wind and the air, she was at one with everything, at one with God." They knew she had to go back to America, the missionary work was calling, but when she went home she wrote saying she would return the following year.

We moved into a beautiful Edwardian house at Harrow on the Hill that summer. It was large enough for my mother to come and live with us. She had her own kitchen and sitting room and bedroom and there were two rooms at the top of the house which became Michael's flat whenever he was home.

We had a large garden with apple and pear trees, part of an old orchard from Victorian days. The road wound up the slope of the hill to end in the churchyard of St. Mary's, with its spire to be seen for miles.

It was a very happy move and the house was full of charm and had a solidity and feeling of character that would be difficult to better. The sitting rooms were very gracious and one had a large arch with pillars at the entrance to the room. All the doors were wide and spacious, made of solid wood in the cross and bible pattern and the downstairs wainscots were at least a foot deep. We all loved the house and it was a delight to have NanNan with us who seemed happy and able to be independent of us when she wished.

On the 30th September that year our telephone's insistent ringing woke me in the early hours. I stumbled downstairs and lifted the receiver. An American voice said, "This is Casandra's brother, I can't get hold of Michael, can you tell him when you think its best to do so – tell him – Casandra is with the Lord! She was killed in a light plane crash over Hawaii today – we don't know the details other than she was asked to take a trip to fly over the volcano. Give Michael our love and tell him we all share this terrible loss."

I went back to bed for a while and tried to sleep but knew I would have to ring Canford at breakfast time. Ray woke and we had our usual morning tea, I told him of the phone call – we were so sad; that lovely girl gone and we knew it must hurt Michael very badly.

I left a message with Judith for him to ring me, also one at the music school – he told me afterwards that he thought NanNan had died and rushed to the telephone to ring home. I said, "Its Casandra", we wept together as I repeated Doug's phone call, he said he would ring her home and parents, he said he was holding the beautiful sea shell she had sent him from America.

We have a copy of the letter he wrote to her parents.

The Elms,
Canford School.
Dear Mr. and Mrs. Ward,

I write to express my deepest sympathy for you and the rest of the family at this time of suffering in the loss of our dear Casandra. I was deeply shocked and grieved by the news so kindly relayed by Doug and such has been the response of my colleagues and friends in Wimborne and Canford that I enclose their words of sympathy with my own.

As you will no doubt realise, Casandra and I drew very close in the time she was in Wimborne. We spent a holiday together and I shared with her my family and music and time, and above all our prayer life. However, such was her spiritual maturity, she acted as a catalyst to my faith and produced wonderful results in such little time. I owe her my strength in Christ which has been given a magnificent purpose in our recent loss.

The witness that has been possible is amazing. So many people saw Christ in her. It is not difficult to see God moving in all this. Never has anyone been more ready to be brought to Christ's Kingdom.

My heartfelt response has been to acclaim how much she must have achieved in Hawaii. She may have lacked an earthly home - and often I helped her to feel rooted in the gentle and lovely Dorset country in which I live - but truly her home was universal - wherever He took her. Her obedience was stunning and peaceful, never assumed. Her thoughtfulness and service an amazing lesson. She was the greatest person I have ever known. I hope that you, too, will know that she is far, far closer to us now.

I rejoice in God's miraculous plan and hope that you too can grow in peace to feel His hand. I think of Casandra at the top of Cwm Rhondda, a Welsh mountain at the head of a valley, standing with arms spread wide, worshipping across the distant landscapes, singing her praises and adoration in response to the power of creation, into the wind. She must have been in such a mood on St. Michael's Day as she flew over Hawaii.

How remarkable that my Bible reading said, "The angels must have carried her away in a vision of ecstasy." How great her work must have been, for her to finish it so soon.

I feel I know you and love you, so please forgive the length and depth of this letter. I would love to take up Doug's offer of a visit if only to talk and pray with you.

Michael

Texas Nov 18th '77

Dear Michael,

At long last I can get a letter to you, I haven't written to anyone else yet. Mainly it seems that the Lord is using Casandra's death in mightier ways than her life. Well, the glory is to Him, Casandra and I talked about you every time we were together, or over the phone. She loved being with you, thought the world of you and liked your parents so much.

I think the one thing that stands out in my memory of talking about you is your sense of humour, Casandra appreciated it so much. We often got silly together, so many people she knew just never laughed. Besides your happy times together she loved your music, your sense of the beautiful. I marvel at how well you understood her. She was not easy to understand nor always easy to get along with.

You are right about her "home" - just any home wouldn't have done, she has the epitome of homes now, one her Father built for her. In the meantime you are young and have all your life ahead of you. You need to find out what the Lord wants you to do. He has a special task for your life and I hope its when our paths may cross and we can see each other some time.

We still think there's a chance the Lord wants us in England. Much of our ministry is over, the ministry we shared with Casandra, now its a drastic change for all of us. Casandra loved England, more than any country in which she lived and was anxious to get back.

We shall first be busy here, and get our Christian heads back on us and remember the body is like an old sack of clothes no longer needed. She's alive, but needs the body no longer so its not important. Perhaps when she comes back with the saints to reign and rule with Him it will be in England. We'll just let the Lord lead and see where we all end up.

Thank you for your lovely letter, we are disappointed we missed your call. It was sweet of you to give Doug's little Jessica the tea set. Casandra had shown it to me when she was home. She loved it and it will mean a lot to Jessica one day from Michael and her aunt and Godmother. I want to send you something of Casandra's and will get to it one of these days. I'll pray over what I should send you and get it off to you.

I did notice in glancing at her notes and calendar that she had the Wales trip marked off and how fabulous it was. We know all things work for good for those who love the Lord and we wouldn't want it any other way. We can only trust Him but that's not always easy.

Came across a poem the other day of a plane ride - threat of danger for a moment, fear and then flight up and beyond the veil with Him.

Thanks again for your sharing and loving letter, send more, we love you and thank you for making her stay in England perfect.

Jean and Duane Ward

In a few weeks they sent Casandra's Bible with all her writings and markings in the margins, bookmarks, little pieces of paper with quotations, etc. What a dear and lovely thing to send him, and then a letter from her brother Doug.

Texas '78

Dear Michael,

Time has really slipped by and I wanted to get this off to you. No telling what kind of letter this will turn out to be. Words are difficult to come up with.

We are resuming 'normal living' again, if ever we did lead a normal life. We are beginning to go through Casandra's things, its going to take me some time to realise just what has happened, just seems to me she's on another trip, well, that's one way to look at it.

Some details you might like to know, I'd like to share. Casandra spent her last month really searching for answers from what has been shared with us by her room-mate - home, husband, loneliness, future - God gave her an answer which she circled on her calendar - the 29th September - "Something special is going to happen to me today, my day of Victory."

On that day of the crash Mr. Bracey was going flying with his wife in order to go see the erupting volcano. Mrs. Bracey was too caught up with work and could not go, she just 'happened' to bump into Casandra, mentioned this and Casandra's instant response was, "I'd love to go in your place." As the Bracey's were close friends this was O.K.'d by Mr. Bracey and away they went.

Casandra was free that morning (miracle of miracles). They crashed that afternoon in the Volcano's National Park - 40 miles from the active cone. The Federal Aviation Association report although not complete, feels that Mr. Bracey because of lack of experience, suffered from vertigo and got lost in the clouds. The impact of the crash was tremendous, as they went into the trees at full power with full tanks of petrol. Death was instant. God was so wonderfully merciful, it was an easy death - probably the easiest. A few things have been found - most were lost, the bodies were burned.

The service in Hawaii was called a Coronation Celebration which matched Casandra's favourite scripture, Psalm 45. Mom and Dad had a Memorial Service in Lubbock, Texas for family and friends and from all accounts the Lord's name was glorified. Mom just said that if vertigo was Mr. Bracey's problem, they both never saw the ground nor had a sense of falling until they hit the ground.

You know Michael, I really praise God that Casandra got to know you and love you, of all her friends you were the dearest. You understood so much of her and so many of her needs. You were so giving and loving. We love you.

I am going to sign off now. Remember how much we love you and are looking forward to seeing you again one day - the Lord only knows.

> *In Jesus,*
> *Doug*

Michael and the Minster Choir gave an Evensong in Salisbury Cathedral soon after this terrible event. I travelled there by train.

We met in the Square and talked and talked. I was overwhelmed by his positive attitude and that he seemed to be filled with an inner joy. How Ray and I had worried, fearing his faith would be hurt, but his faith was stronger. I've often thought of it since and understood, in the light of our own experience.

He motored me to the station via Stonehenge, where we watched the sun go down in that magical atmosphere of half light, the dramatic shape of those stones and the eternal quality of love we felt for each other. He was always to feel sorrow and yet joy for the time given to him with Casandra and we could sense his maturity and growth through those months.

When I returned home I delved into my Shell Guide book and found quite a lot about Stonehenge, including a line from a poem by Wordsworth where he called it: *inmate of lonesome nature's endless year*. In a letter to Michael I quoted a paragraph from the Guide:

> *... all by itself in the wide sheep walk and cornfields of the Plain, yet mysterious and suggestive, small in such immensity, England's chief symbol of remotest and most enigmatic antiquity.*

I remember writing that one could imagine how ancient man thought the stones actually contained the sun – as though God, come to earth in a blaze of light.

~·~·~·~·~·~·~

Canford School has a remarkably good music department and there were golden opportunities to arrange concerts, to give recitals and to accompany the voices and young instrumentalists of the school as well as the visiting artists. One such privilege was to be at the piano for a lecture recital given by the famous clarinettist Jack Brymer. When it came to an encore, he flung Michael a piece of music which he sight-read a most tricky and flashy little piece, very difficult, but he carried it off with aplomb. He was now a seasoned performer.

Watching him conduct the school choir and orchestra in a performance of the Messiah, then the Blandford Choral Society in St. John's Passion in Blandford Parish Church were unforgettable times.

He seemed to inspire a sense of 'giving of their best' in his musicians, they loved him and he was able to draw out of them what he felt the composer needed. I think he was able to pass on to them many of Dr. George Thalben-Ball's insights into the words and music that he had so deeply inherited and that were so important and made him such a good choir trainer. No wonder he received the choir training diploma from the Royal College of Organists at that time.

A Western Gazette newspaper critic wrote:

Michael James drew some captivatingly quiet singing from the choir, notably in the unaccompanied "Sanctus". This was a thoroughly worthwhile presentation, meticulously prepared under the leadership of a first class musician.

He had many private pupils as well as teaching at the advanced level of 'A' music at Canford, and of course always the commitment of the Assistant Organist at the Minster with Mr. Christopher Dowie as the organist.

The organ is a very fine "Walker". Michael accompanied the choir at most of the services with Christopher conducting. He played a series of great works for voluntaries, playing sometimes for at least a quarter of an hour before the main Eucharist Service, always trying to enhance the worship of the congregation and matching the music to the words and events of the church's year.

The Reverend Douglas Strickland was the incumbent at that time, a man of warmth and understanding. He shared with Michael a very jolly sense of humour and would enjoy the addition of a few little, discreet hopping and skipping bars of music as he processed to the high altar or back, as well as the deeply felt moments of wonder and holiness in the worship. Very often, there were many members of the congregation crowding round the organ console to hear the last of the Voluntary following the service. He was much loved and appreciated.

There came a time when he felt that he should change course and though keeping his many private pupils and continuing as Assistant Organist at the Minster, he resigned his post at Canford School to enable him to have more time to practise, to receive organ lessons from Gillian Weir, and to become more of a recitalist.

Michael wrote:

I am waiting to leave here with alert sensitivity to the luxury of the place and the textures and smells, but with the knowledge that I am doing what must be done! My mind is breaking through like Spring and I'm so glad. "Bury the old problems," came to me as I played today and all was released and relaxed playing. How different I am from the "boy" who came to teach four years ago. I've met death and life, the reality of my own priorities and standards and competence in administration; the future is exciting – "What will He have me do?

So in July 1978 he left The Elms at Canford School and took lodgings in Wimborne, in various places, but for a few months with 'Jimmy James', the photographer at the Royal Studios in East Street.

It was to prove a noisy road and he found it difficult to concentrate on his music so he moved out to a beautiful thatched cottage on the green at Sturminster Marshall. A garden full of old apple trees, the river running along the back and the water meadows beyond. A spiral staircase led to his bedroom, large and with a high pitched ceiling under the thatch. A huge beam went across the room at shoulder height so it had to be ducked under quite frequently. It was the loveliest place to be.

We received a letter from Judith Marriott at this time.

My dear Margaret and Ray,

I want to tell you that Martin and I could not be more behind Michael in his recent decision. For many reasons it is a courageous decision, but I have no doubt whatsoever that it is a right one, and if the facts didn't convince me, I would only have to look at him to know that he has done the best thing for him.

I have never known him look more at peace, more tranquil or happier. He has grown in stature, he is truly following his own conviction and looks a new man as a result. My first reaction was one of huge relief for him, that a large elastic band that had been restricting him was now broken and he is about to grow and be enabled to be far more fulfilled.

How wonderful too that he is not going altogether but will be nearby and still able to come to Blandford Choral Society - which for me is hugely important. At the same time as feeling all this genuinely, there is of course the other side, our side and the school's side will sustain an enormous loss.

There is no denying our community will have a large hole - the Music School will lose its heart and soul and though I know we won't lose a friend, it will not be quite the same. Michael brings so much - himself - to so many Canford gatherings and occasions and though we have many lovely people in our community - people of Michael's quality do not come around often enough to feel we can lightly lose a friend from our midst.

It will be wonderful to follow his doings and he knows that always we will be behind him in whatever he does and want him to feel that we will help him in any way we can. I know his inner resources are immense and times like this prove it.

This was going to be a few lines, and even now I've only written a little of what we feel. I wanted to tell you that we admire him more than I can possibly say - he is indeed special. We hope to see you when you are next in Wimborne.

With love

Judith

This was a wonderful letter to receive and so very kind of her to write it.

Michael had spent four years teaching at Canford but now his career blossomed and the very first thing to happen was a scholarship to attend a summer organ course in Holland and then a fortnight in Venice.

His Holland visit was full of activity, he played on the famous St. Baavo organ in Haarlem and an album was filled with postcards of the glorious organ cases and pipes at Amsterdam and Rotterdam. During the fortnight in Venice he studied with Roberto Micconi, the organist of St. Marks.

Michael wrote:

What a great Cathedral of magnificent acoustic, mosaics and spirituality! Historically, this huge building with its continuous high choir galleries, inspired composers to write dramatic, spacious music to be sounded in all corners of the church; choirs calling, answering, echoing, competing and joining in magnificent symbolism and praise. I was allowed unlimited practice on beautifully restored 18th century organs which led to the privilege of playing for Mass at St. Marks and giving two recitals, one in Vivaldi's own church and one where Monteverdi is buried. In Venice one is surrounded by great art, the constant reminder is, how highly the music compliments the visual arts in worship as a means to glorify God, express our feelings and make our witness obvious.

In the Minster magazine he wrote:

Having just returned from Venice and also attending the Three Choirs Festival at Gloucester, I was inspired again by the dramatic and visual care in the presentation of worship. However, I often came away from the various churches I have visited for worship since my return, disappointed in the congregational speaking and singing. For me all the varied schemes held a common lesson. When we perform an Act of Worship, it requires as much effort and preparation as would an act of a play – more in fact, because our worship reaches beyond fiction in response to the living relationship at the heart of our faith. How impressive and how rare the fine example of clear speaking, disciplined and heartfelt joining in prayers and words of the hymns, which in one church produced an impressive unity of choir, organist, congregation and Clergy.

In Venice he met Jürgen and Elizabeth Schwab both organists from Stuttgart, who invited him to give a recital in the Hospitalkirke in the spring of 1980. He began to prepare for a concert he'd arranged in the Wessex Hall, Poole for March 1980 in which he would conduct Brahms German Requiem with combined Dorset choirs and orchestra and be soloist for Mozart's Piano Concerto in D minor.

All the winter of '79 he was preparing and learning the concerto and had piano lessons from Anthea Cohen in London and organ lessons from Gillian Weir in Cambridge. He trained the choirs for the Brahms and by Christmas he was feeling well forward in his plans.

We spent Christmas with him, borrowing Richard and Annabelle Willett's Georgian house at Spetisbury, the two members of his Trio!

On Christmas Eve there was a severe frost and every twig and branch shone white. Coming out of the Minster in the early morning and driving back to Spetisbury in moonlight was a magical ride – oh! how we loved Dorset! Ray had to be back on Boxing Day for the performance of the Ice Pantomime at Wembley Arena, so we saw him off at Bournemouth Station and then went down to the Pier and walked along the front in the gale and were caught in the spray from the rough sea, tearing itself to pieces on the beach. Then there was torrential rain.

Michael was driving me to meet Major and Mrs. Cardozo and their family whom he had recently met. They lived near Shaftesbury. As we motored north we came across severe flooding and many times had to drive through quite high water in the lanes. We reached West Orchard safely but then couldn't leave and the Cardozos put us up for the night.

I could see why Michael had become so fond of the family. Music played a large part in their lives. Dominic was a violin maker in his spare time and his wife Ursula had been a ballet dancer before her marriage. They now had four grown up children, Clare a music teacher, Anna who sang, Charles a lover of opera and Catherine who was to study music at Durham University. When they were together they played instruments and sang and they had formed a lovely friendship with Michael who was drawn into the family with love and warmth. It was so good to be part of their Christmas celebrations and to be asked to stay the night, too. Their hospitality was warm indeed. Clare was to become a special friend of Michael's and now of ours, a friendship that has grown through the years.

The next morning the floods had abated and we set off back to London. We talked of the end of the decade and what the eighties would hold in store for us. I said that there was always a little trepidation mixed with the excitement of a new year – one didn't know what was ahead and how good it was not to know. Michael said that with one's hand in God's, every situation could be faced with confidence. Little did we know how soon that statement would be tested.

The concert at Poole was scheduled for March 21st and nearer to that time Michael showed me a fairly large lump that he had discovered in his left armpit but he said he wouldn't do anything about it until the concert was over as his music mustn't be interrupted at that stage.

Looking back I don't think I worried about it, and certainly Michael didn't, he was far too busy.

We travelled to Poole with my Mother in a friend's car, had a picnic on the way and snow was falling when we reached Poole.

The Wessex Hall was very full for the concert and the large choir and orchestra filled the stage. First of all Grant Bocking conducted the choir in Mozart's Ave Verum and then Michael walked on to the platform to perform the piano concerto; it was good to hear and see his confidence, it was as though he had been playing concertos for years.

It was a beautiful performance and much applauded and appreciated by the audience and the choir. Then he returned to conduct the Requiem. He gathered the orchestra and choir together and produced an overwhelming sound.

The Bournemouth Evening Echo critic, Ken Williams, wrote on 26th March 1980:–

> *Michael James at once established what a fluent and musicianly pianist he is. There was great rhythmic strength and lyrical beauty in the solo playing in the performance of Mozart's Piano Concerto in D Minor. The Brahms German Requiem is essentially a personal expression of belief in death as a state of blissfully peaceful eternal rest. Thanks largely to Michael James, returning to the platform to conduct, with his clear understanding of the overall design of the work and the authority with which he persuaded his large forces to conform to it, the overwhelming feeling, left at the end of the performance was one of consolation and hope.*

He then travelled to Stuttgart to give an organ recital at the Hospitalkirke and to stay with Jürgen and Elizabeth.

Here were two younger people living the same kind of life, deeply committed Christians, music in their very souls and TRAIN enthusiasts!! A model railway under the piano and round the edge of the room with locos, trucks and carriages!

It was a splendid week for them all. Jürgen wrote later that as they watched Michael's plane leaving to return to England, their eyes filled with tears to see such a wonderful friend leaving them.

They had felt such peace and loving during his visit that their longed for conception of a child was at last achieved – a child who was to be Michael's Godson.

~.~.~.~.~.~.~.~

Rochester Cathedral

Far Horizons

Michael viewed the fact of having to go into hospital to have the lymph gland removed from his armpit as purely an interruption in his music making.

They discovered it was cancerous and a further small operation to search for any tissue left behind was performed shortly after and proved negative. There followed extensive scans and X-rays, but nothing was found in any other part of his body and he was pronounced healthy. The specialists said they would need to check him with tests every three months for ten years and then would prove him clear of cancer. Ten years seemed such a long time and with hope and optimism and acceptance of the whole idea as being a minor interruption, he gave another recital only five days after the last operation, feeling no affects or stiffness at all.

The next few weeks he carried on as busily as before, spending every twenty four hours as though they were forty-eight hours!

We asked him to take as much rest as he could and he seemed relaxed. He gave several talks to the boys at Canford and also at Bryanston School on being diagnosed with cancer and his Christian viewpoint on acceptance.

Ray booked a week's holiday at a cottage in East Dean near Birling Gap in Sussex and we drove down the first week in September, stopping at the famous Ditchling Beacon on the Downs for our coffee; we reached the cottage at lunchtime. It was glorious weather and a perfect week, Michael driving to and fro, giving recitals and taking the opportunity to visit Glyndebourne.

We walked one night down to Birling Gap and saw the beach under a great canopy of stars. We walked up the hill to the cottage where we had stayed so many times when he was a small boy and together we watched that small figure come through the gate and go proudly by, down towards the sea with his bucket and spade. We were filled with joy for ourselves as part of all creation.

The last evening we lingered at the Gap to watch the sunset, a superb Turner colouring of the sky, cliffs, beach and foam. Ray asked Michael to stand looking out to sea while he took a photograph so as to mask the sun shining straight into the lens, Michael's figure was in silhouette, the sun behind him and sinking fast. We waited 'til the sun had gone below the horizon then we started home.

Getting back to Dorset he had a new address. The Governors of the Minster had rented a small house to Michael, at a peppercorn rent; during that summer the river had flooded and the cottage at Sturminster Marshall had several inches of water over the ground floor. Luckily nothing was damaged, as all his music had been carried upstairs at the first warning, so back he moved to Wimborne.

The house was just five minutes walk from the Minster, it contained a large sitting room, a study to teach in which was big enough for a piano and all his books, and had two bedrooms upstairs. He was realising that the pianos he had been playing were just not good enough, so he decided to launch out with a mortgage and buy himself a second hand 6ft. Steinway. It made a glorious sound and was so rewarding for every subtle nuance of touch, another step forward in his musicality.

In October he entered the West of England Organ Festival at Bristol and we travelled down for the last sequence of classes. He came second in two sections to the winner, a young sixteen year old at Clifton College, a brilliant future musician. The adjudicator, Sir David Wilcocks, spoke of Michael's power to perform, portray and communicate the music to his audience. He gave a wonderful performance of Herbert Howells Paean, how we wish we had a recording of that day.

Christmas we spent at Harrow, Michael driving home after all the services at the Minster and as he said, "Hark the Herald Angels – for the seventh time". His present to me was the Alternative Service Book, he wrote on the inside page, "For my dearest Mother, with love for life in the Eighties." Michael 25.12.80.

On January 17th 1981 he took the Fellowship exam at the Royal College of Organists and passed. It was his third attempt and at last he was a Fellow. We celebrated with a meal and a show in the West End. Ray took photos of him wearing his new hood. It had been his Christmas present. Ray said, "Don't wear it before the exam of course, but this is to tell you, I know you will pass." It was a wonderful moment for Michael, knowing that his Father had so much faith in him.

There were tests to be done at the hospital every few months, but they always proved negative.

In March he received an invitation to go to Chicago, to give the Dame Myra Hess Memorial concert with the young American oboist, Keith Hooper. He booked his flight and I saw him off from Heathrow. A huge Jumbo Jet 747 named Shakespeare, which lifted up from the runway as though a giant hand was under it. It turned slightly towards the west and was gone into the clouds. The eight hour flight was without incident, giving him plenty of time in which to study the music yet again for the forthcoming concerts. He said he had a perfect glimpse of Chicago for the first time as they flew down out of the clouds, 'the vast lake stretching to the horizon and the tower blocks and skyscrapers like a series of pencils standing upright in bright sunshine'.

The broadcast of the Dame Myra Hess Concert was the following day, there was not much time to prepare it together, but it all seemed to work like magic. They played Bach, Telemann, Hindemith and the lovely sonata by Saint Saens for oboe and piano. In the second movement, Saint Saens depicts a lonely hillside where a shepherd is playing his pipe. Keith Hooper's family had originally come from Dorset, where his grandfather had been a shepherd. This extraordinary coincidence gave the two musicians a special rapport and the performance was excellent.

They gave a similar recital in Buffalo, New York State, and of course managed some sightseeing too. A trip to the top of Sear Tower, a visit to a nightclub to hear a coloured man play piano jazz and on St. Patrick's Day, to watch the jubilations and to see the river dyed green!

The three weeks proved to be a marvellous experience, he returned home on March 20th and we drove down to Dorset where he was conducting the Blandford Choral Society in a concert for the Musicians Christian Fellowship in Boscombe. I attended the rehearsal as well as the concert. It was good to hear him rehearsing the choir, giving them word pictures to help them get what he wanted, drawing out from them a musicality together they didn't possess individually.

For the first time I stayed at the new house and I took on the job of altering curtains to make them fit the large windows. We sat the first evening after the concert in the snug little sitting room he had made upstairs next to his bedroom. He had heard some sad news. A good friend, who had only recently been given his own parish in Southampton, had been killed on his motor bike a few days before. We talked of Casandra and now of Christopher Brooks, two friends who had died at about the age of thirty.

Michael said, "Casandra's death I can understand more than Christopher's, he didn't seem to be ready or as though he had grown enough."

"Don't you think that perhaps we go on growing after death", I replied, "I can't think that God would want to take us early, but if death happens in this world where so much chance prevails, God can make the most of the situation and give us work to do with Him".

Michael said that he felt sure that everything was in God's hands, had always been and would always be, that we were all interwoven in the pattern, adding, "Casandra was a shining example, how supreme she had been in showing God's will."

During the interval at that evening concert I had been introduced to the Reverend Norman and Mary Taylor. They had become friends of Michael's this last year. His parish was at West Moors near Wimborne.

I liked them instantly, we found we could speak at depth immediately and they had greeted me with great warmth. They said how much they loved Michael, how they admired him, they spoke of him as though he was a son. Norman remarked that they were on the same spiritual wavelength. I hoped we would meet again as I felt we had a bond between us.

That visit was one I savoured. Every minute with our son was always special. At Eastertime we were back again and this time with NanNan. We had a wonderful four days together.

The three hour service on Good Friday was conducted by the Revd. Preb. Edmund Buxton and Michael played the hymns. Edmund was very moved with the devotional depth of the service and when we said goodbye to him at the gates of the Minster, he put his arm round Michael and drew him close, "My Godson, organist, friend," he said.

We went to a most meaningful service, one that is in the Alternative Service Book for reaffirming one's faith and, of course, on Easter Sunday the Minster was full. NanNan and I sat together listening and absorbing Michael's playing. On our way to the Minster in the car, I had told him that I had that wonderful tune from the Christmas Oratorio, *Mighty Lord* on my brain. I had woken up that morning, that joyous Easter morning with it in my head. We both roared the words and sang at the top of our voices much to NanNan's amusement. When Michael took his seat before the service and began the Voluntary, what should it be but an extemporization of the tune, *Mighty Lord*. How I loved it and praised God for Michael and his gifts.

He drove us later to see the Nine Stones beyond Dorchester. They stood beside the main road with a small wire fence surrounding them and I daresay most people passed them by without a second glance. Compared with Stonehenge, quite minuscule but, nevertheless, most impressive. The stones are about five to six feet tall, in a circle, some reclining. The texture is quite rough. A dense wood of trees about them and wild garlic in bloom around the base. It was a timeless moment to stand with our hands against the rocks and feel the energy of centuries and yet the stillness and the mystery of why they were there.

We found a letter written by Michael a few years ago in which he talked about rocks:

I always find rocks amazing evidence of the heart beat of God. They become what they are so slowly compared with our life span; they belong so much more to the infinite, to wisdom, to truth, beauty and goodness, to the whole slow process of the Universe. Its a wonderful vision to contemplate.

In all the study of how things are, I can never escape the awareness of why. As the time goes by I gain more strength, hope and joy from some of the answers.

From Dorchester we went to Cerne Abbas to see the Giant, cut in the side of the hill. Again a feeling of strength from the past and an endless chain which seems to link us all. Michael drove us through the lovely Dorset lanes and in one village, at the end of the street, was a ford. The water was a few inches deep and had a footbridge delicately poised beside it.

Michael said, "Shall we go through it?" A gleam of childlike joy on his face, mirrored by mine and NanNan's!

He drove through it and we all exclaimed about the chuckling sound of the water around the wheels. He stopped the car a little way on, "Lets go through it again," he said, and so we enjoyed the experience once more.

There were two more recitals to plan after Easter and much preparation for the second concert he was to give in Stuttgart, a return visit, and the looking forward to meeting his Godson Johannes born in January to Jürgen and Elizabeth. He sent us a card from there:

Am riding the train in brilliant sunshine into central Stuttgart for a last rehearsal before tonight's recital, it should go well, it has been widely advertised. The organ is more pleasing this year and reveals to me the weakness of our English organ builders and the ignorance of British experts in the Classical Reform. Johannes is GORGEOUS, loves patterns, lying on my shoulder and looking at a mobile. I've nearly lost my index finger with his sucking it, as a mother substitute. See you on Thursday at Heathrow.

The concert was a success, but later Jürgen told us that Michael had felt a difficulty in his right hand, it hadn't seemed as fluent as it should be but otherwise it was as brilliant as before. He said, "What is amazing is the colours he uses, it is an inspiration to hear him play."

They decided to travel to the Alps, a few hours train journey, so as to ascend the Zuggspittze. Three different trains take one to the top; a cable type for the second and then the third inside the mountain on a kind of ratchet system. Anyway, at the summit, at 9,000 ft. a hotel, and of all things, a telephone! The phone rang at home, lunchtime. It was Michael from the top of the mountain. He said how exhilarating the journey had been, how rarified the air seemed, there was no view from the top as they were in cloud, but it was wonderful: he would be home as planned the next day. I was thrilled with our short talk.

As we learned later, they started down the mountain and Michael felt a strange sensation in his right arm, a sense of the muscles all vibrating but his arm was still. The sensation was violent and they thought that maybe it was because of the lack of oxygen at that height. A doctor was called by the train guard and at the first station Michael and Jürgen were taken to the local hospital where he was given a thorough check for a suspected heart attack. But they found nothing wrong.

They caught the next train back to Stuttgart. The next day another of those strange sensations occurred in his arm but nothing more. He caught the plane home and I met him at Heathrow. I thought he looked very tired but he was relaxed and happy and so full of joy at seeing the views from the Zuggspittze once they came below the clouds and he had taken several photos which were still inside the camera.

The next day he went to Rochester Cathedral for an interview. We had heard previously that he had been short-listed for the post of Assistant Organist, there. He had a thrilling day, a short training of the choir and he was able to use the picture image of the cable car going up the mountain for a point he wanted to make with the boys. There were interviews with the Dean and Precentor and other clergy and, of course, with Barry Ferguson, the organist.

He came home about six thirty and at seven the phone rang, it was the Dean, offering him the job. We could hardly believe it and Michael even discussed with us for a short while whether he should accept. But it was the work he had always wanted to do and he and Barry would make a good team again and renew a long friendship.

He decided to take us to Rochester the next day, Sunday, so we set off early to be there in good time. In fact the roads were not good and full of traffic and we went through a cloudburst. The rain poured in torrents on to the car and slowed us up.

We arrived at the Cathedral after the Service had begun but, nevertheless, we were in time to take Communion together. When the choir processed out, they all spotted Michael and were nodding and grinning in turn, obviously very pleased to see him and glad that it was he who had been chosen as Assistant.

We all met for coffee in the community centre beside the Cathedral. It had originally been the Deanery, a beautiful Georgian house with a large garden, a huge magnolia tree trained against one wall. Barry was very pleased to see us again, we had met Dean John Arnold several years before at Forest Hill, where he had been a young curate: he and Michael had become friends then and it seemed another good coincidence.

Going home in the car Michael said how young the clergy team were and what an exciting atmosphere they generated. He would have to move there in August for his work would commence in September. But now it was May, and it seemed an ideal amount of time in which slowly to wind up his work in Wimborne at the Minster, arrange for someone to take over his pupils and the Blandford Choral Society, in fact he was already training a young man to conduct the choir should he find himself moving from Dorset.

Rochester was so entirely different from Wimborne – in which he had lived and loved and played and taught for the last seven years; but only a month or two previously he had been made Director and Conductor of Milton Abbey Festival, so every year he would be able to return to Dorset.

Rochester is the Cathedral, its precincts, its old High Street with Dickensian shops, the Castle in half ruins and the River Medway. Apart from these it is an industrial city and as Michael said, "The Cathedral and its environs are so beautiful one needs the proximity of the town to keep ones feet on the ground."

He would need to live as near the Cathedral as possible but a flat or apartment would have to be found, as there was no 'tied' property for the Assistant. The organist's house is No. 7 Minor Canon Row, a Georgian row of terrace houses in the Close and it would have been nice to think of Michael living somewhere there. However, we all said it was the place for him to be and God would be sure to have provided the accommodation as well, and it would soon be revealed.

He motored back to Wimborne and spread his good news to everyone, but it wasn't really good news for them, they were going to lose their friend and teacher, a sensitive and loving musician and they were not sure he could be replaced. Loving as they were though, in return, they were also glad for him for it was a big step in his career.

Some of those strange feelings were occurring in his arm again, once or twice they became quite strong and moved up into the side of his face. A sensation of muscles out of control and trembling. He decided to ring Mark Kissin, the doctor at Northwick Park Hospital, who, on hearing the symptoms asked him to go and see him. Mark told us later, "My heart sank when he told me, I guessed what was the trouble."

It was May 21st and we were waiting for Michael to arrive home, he had decided to come up on the coach. The journey takes much longer that way. He telephoned us from Heathrow to say he was there and was catching the bus to bring him to Harrow. Ray was going into work but he said he would wait and see Michael. So conscientious where work was concerned, to put off going, just to see Michael and be late for his students was unheard of. How glad we were afterwards, that he had obeyed some instinct and stayed at home.

It was pouring with rain and we stood by the window and waited for him: at last about 2 o'clock we saw him, wet and dishevelled. He came in almost distraught. We gave him a towel to dry his hair and it was most odd to see him so upset. He had been travelling five hours he said, he left Wimborne at nine, what a ridiculous way to travel. He was so cross, but he calmed down as I gave him a late lunch. Then he said, "Excuse me, I must go to the toilet", he went upstairs and we heard a strangled cry of "Help me", then the noise of him falling. We flew up the stairs.

He was lying on the landing outside the bathroom door having a seizure, his right leg and arm were jerking, he was going blue in the face, gasping for breath, then violently jerking all over. Ray held his hand, I loosened his ties and clothes, then ran to the phone to dial 999. The slow deliberate voice asking for my name and address maddened me, "An ambulance quickly", I cried desperately and was asked to repeat the address again. It was an age before the voice said an ambulance would be sent. I could hear Michael making terrible noises in his throat trying to breathe but he was unconscious and Ray was holding him when I ran back.

Slowly the convulsions subsided and he began to breathe normally, he appeared to be asleep. Ray called that the ambulance was arriving, those few minutes had seemed like hours.

As I heard them come upstairs Michael opened his eyes, "The ambulance is here, its alright, darling."

"Ambulance," he murmured, "what for?"

The two attendants, a man and a woman, wrapped him in a blanket in a small chair, and carried him down. We grabbed coats and keys and went with him. On our way to the hospital, only five minutes from the house by road, Michael seemed to remember what had happened, he spoke to us and smiled. We went straight to the casualty department, he was wheeled into a small room, the doors were shut, and there we were, our faces hot and deep red, hearts beating fast, but he was alive. I thought he was dying on the floor upstairs at home and I had never seen anything so horrific before.

Mark Kissin came into Casualty from Fleming Ward and saw Michael for a while, then came over to talk to us in reception. "It is very grave I think," he said, "he may have neurological cancer, anyway we will keep him in for tests and give him a drug that will stop him having any more fits at the moment."

So – so –, last year's tests after the operation had all proved negative, we had such high hopes that he was cured but it was not to be, cancer had reared its ugly head again. Oh! our beloved Michael, our only son, our dear, dear boy!

We stayed a long time and he was finally taken upstairs to Fleming Ward where he had been last year for those small operations to remove the lymph gland.

It was decided that he should have a course of Radio Therapy, as the X-rays proved that he had several quite extensive small growths on the left side of his brain, which affected his right side and had caused the convulsion. It was explained as Jacksonian Epilepsy.

He stayed in Fleming Ward for three days and although he was tired and taking several tablets each day, he seemed quite well. The Radio Therapy was to be given him at Mount Vernon Hospital and would commence the following week. The specialist told him that he would have a one in three chance of the treatment being successful and did he wish to continue with a heavy drug programme awhile and put off the therapy 'til later? Michael decided that he would go ahead with it now. He was completely unafraid and said he was quite ready to die, but how were we going to manage? We must talk and talk together.

In one conversation Ray said, "Now we know what it is we know what to fight."

Michael's answer was, "If it is my time to die, I could be going against God's will to fight."

He decided that if I could be spared for three days he would like me to accompany him down to Wimborne to collect music and correspondence, but, chiefly, to collect the music he wished to study through the two weeks of Radio Therapy. It was going to be a question of spending a few moments each morning at the hospital and the rest of the time would be free. The specialist told him that they never knew how each patient would be affected by the treatment, everyone reacted differently so he could work as much as he wanted or rest each day accordingly.

We thought the visit to Wimborne was essential for him so we set off on Wednesday, May 27th. It was actually my birthday, but I had hardly noticed that it was. Michael had ordered some slides for me of the pictures sent back from Voyager, of Saturn and Jupiter, but they hadn't arrived, his card was beautiful and in the light of events had deep meaning. It was a reproduction of F.W. Bourdillon, *The Jubilee Hat*. A mother showing a hat she had made for the Jubilee. Michael wrote inside:

The hat we all three sewed when I was so big! The hat I'm at last about to put on, is now in my hands - praise be - definitely a Cathedral Organists hat.

A very Happy Birthday - lots of love - Michael.

We drove to Wimborne quickly and easily and spent two days packing up boxes, washing and ironing and generally leaving the house in perfect order. He was happy and content and very relaxed. There were many people he had to see or telephone but in an extraordinary way, the phone rang with just the very person at the other end to whom he wished to speak.

One call came to ask him to look at a particular organ to see if it was a 'good buy'. A complete stranger had been given his number to ring. Michael apologised for not being able to help, he explained he was to have a spell of treatment. "I'm sorry to hear that", said the stranger, "at what hospital will you be?" He then went on to say that Mount Vernon was a fine place, he knew the Radio Therapy Unit for it was there that he had been Chaplain. Michael said, "God is here with me and is seeing me through every minute of the day."

On Ascension Day, in the afternoon, we drove to West Moors to see Norman and Mary Taylor. I stayed with Mary and told her all that had happened. Michael went into the study with Norman, they prayed together and then went to the church where Norman anointed him with oil. We prayed in the house at the same time and we wept together as a great surge of trust enveloped us. We knew Michael was in God's hands. They arrived back from the church and in the vicarage kitchen, Michael clasped me in his arms whilst we cried for Joy. I write it purposely with a capital letter. It was one of the greatest moments of our lives. Whatever happened we knew Michael would be taken care of in a special way.

We left after tea to go on to the Minster for the Ascension Day Eucharist, I sat on the organ seat with him. He played as he had never played before. Each note – each phrase – a paean of praise. The whole choir was watching him in astonishment, the congregation were lifted up with wonder, the hymns were glorious to hear. A prayer was said for Michael and at the time of Communion we walked up to the Altar together and alone – everyone waited until we reached the Altar rail first – nothing arranged – just a strange "something" that happened.

The Voluntary after the service was by Messiaen, *Transports de Joie*. The composer quotes the liturgy of the day, "Let us give thanks to God the Father who has made us worthy to partake in the inheritance of the Saints of Light and has raised us up and given us a place in heaven in Jesus Christ," He played it most gloriously, everyone stayed to listen, it was pure inspiration. We were not to know that it was the last time he was going to give his praise and worship on this Earth. What sort of music and what instruments he would be able to play in the next life I can only imagine and I often try to think of it, but he must be making wonderful music for God, otherwise he would not have been taken.

We didn't talk much together, there was just a quietness and acceptance and there were many practical things to be done. He had a little bell by his bedside to ring if he needed me in the night. We were never sure if he might have another attack, but the tablets seemed to be doing their work and except for a few little trembles in his right arm he was quite alright. We packed the car with everything he thought he would need and before setting out he sat at the Steinway Grand and played some Brahms and Chopin, "How good it sounds and how glad I am to have bought it. It is wonderful to have had this time here", he said "thank you for giving it to me. I feel I am going through a spring cleaning – both physically and mentally to prepare me for the new job at Rochester. Already the house and my papers are in order."

We drove away, taking the minor roads home instead of the motorway. It was a beautiful afternoon, warm and sunny. We stopped for a while at Alresford to see the engines and rolling stock of the Watercress Line. There were several engines there in the sheds. Two already beautifully restored and others in various states of disrepair. They looked magnificent when restored to their former glory, we wandered along beside them, the wheels much taller than me. We vowed to return in the summer when the trains would be running. I remember the bright colours, the reds, the shiny blacks, the gleaming brass and the powerful look of the pistons.

We left there reluctantly and drove slowly on until we came to a very nice looking old Inn near Newbury. We had a plateful of delicious chicken and chips and vegetables, washed down with long lemon and limes. We sat at a little table and held hands quite unselfconsciously. The strong bond between us could never be severed whatever would happen in the future. He looked at me with contented love, we shared so much, he was not just a son but a deep friend.

We arrived back at Harrow in the evening, Ray came in from College soon after and we told him all that had happened over the last three days. We decided that we would visit Rochester again the next day.

We rang Barry Ferguson who suggested that Michael should play the Canticles and that it would be a special service, for a new honorary Canon would be installed at Evensong. Who should it be, but the Reverend John Hargreaves, Edmund Buxton's brother-in-law. So there we were at Rochester with the Buxton and Hargreaves families and Michael playing the organ there for the first time in his capacity as Assistant Organist Elect.

Rochester was bedecked with bunting for the Dickens' Festival. We watched a parade in the High Street and had a picnic lunch in the garden of the Close, many people were in Victorian fancy dress. The Service was impressive, Edmund and Katharine sat with us in the choir stalls – the curtain at the organ seat was drawn slightly apart and we glanced several times upwards to watch Michael there. He was standing a lot of the time while Barry played.

Afterwards Edmund climbed the steep stairs to the organ loft to speak to Michael. He warmly clasped him in his arms and said he would always be in his prayers and especially through these next weeks of treatment.

There was tea in the crypt to follow and we met the other clergy including Bishop Say. They were all so pleased that Michael was going to be with them in September and also teaching at the Kings School and delighted that he would take the name of Rochester with him abroad when he gave future recitals. He had a long talk with the Precentor about the Monteverdi Vespers which he would be conducting at Milton Abbey and they discussed how little we know of Mary in the Scriptures. "We don't magnify the Lord enough," Michael said, "as Mary did. If we were only like the glass that you can put close to the ground, so directing the heat of the sun's rays, as to make that spot of light burst into flame; if only we were that glass, our lives would shine with God's purpose, we would be a continual praise, aflame with God's glory."

~*~*~*~*~*~*~*~

Harrow on the Hill

I t had been a fabulous day in Rochester full of special things, we call them coincidences, but Michael's life has been full of many such times, which he called 'God's coincidences'. We would go on, wondering and marvelling but in fact it was obvious that he felt close to God.

On Monday, June 1st, an ambulance came for him at 9.15 a.m. He asked me to go with him, a first sign of nervousness. He didn't want to be with strangers on that first day of treatment, and I did go each time over the two weeks.

We arranged for our neighbour, Celia, to drive us in Michael's car. We were at Mount Vernon for such a short time on those therapy visits and the ambulance would wait two hours before returning. The first treatment consisted of one minute under the huge Radio Therapy machine, directed to the left side of his head above the ear.

We had a taxi home and in the quarter of an hour it took to

do the journey he was beginning to have a headache. I put the folding bed out, downstairs in the sitting room and he laid down, shivering and perspiring, his head now filled with severe pain. We rang the hospital and Sister suggested he had two Disprin. He took them and soon slept for about an hour and a half. When he awoke the headache had almost gone but he was exhausted and stayed in bed some time.

From the symptoms and the way he described them it sounded to me like a very bad type of sun or heat stroke. Although he was so hot, he needed a hot water bottle to keep him from shivering. He felt well enough later to get up and eat quite a good meal; we talked gently and listened to records.

He had four treatments the first week and each day the after effects were less severe, but on the second or third day, I don't remember which, his head was aching badly. I leant down to the bed and held his head in my hands. I could feel a huge pulse in my fingers, we prayed together and some words from the Eucharist came into my mind. I said aloud:

> *We are not worthy to gather up the crumbs under Thy table, but Thou art the same Lord whose nature is always to have mercy. Grant us therefore, gracious Lord, so to eat the flesh of Thy dear Son, Jesus Christ, and to drink His blood, that our sinful bodies may be made clean by His body and our souls washed through His most precious blood and that we may evermore dwell in Him and He in us. Amen.*

Michael smiled and said quite gently and quietly, "The pain has gone."

I took my hands away from his head. "The huge pulsing

throb you were having", I said, "I could feel it right through my fingers."

He replied that he hadn't been aware of a throb, only an ache and we realised that the pulse was in my own hands. The few subsequent times I was able to help him in this way, my hands always felt this huge throbbing. We agreed it must be the energy of God's healing.

As the days went by we got to know the other patients. Most were elderly or middle-aged, but a few were young. One boy was bald, his face was puffy and white and he looked extremely ill. We were told that Michael would lose his hair so he was fitted with a wig. Although he said he wouldn't mind being bald, it would be three or four months before the hair grew again, so perhaps for other people's sake he should wear a wig.

Certainly for concerts and also teaching, but during the two weeks there was no sign of his hair falling out. He was tired and at times quite well, but his hearing troubled him. He kept hearing a kind of metallic sound, and women's voices sounded higher. He could not stand loud noises but he sat at the piano many days and studied the score of *The Dream of Gerontious* by Elgar. The work was to be performed in the summer, also Faure's Requiem which he would conduct at Milton Abbey.

Ray brought some books on Elgar from the College Library and we walked to Harrow library to borrow records. He designed a paper poster heading for the Milton Abbey Festival, one which they still use, and there were all sorts of arrangements to be made, the secretary rang frequently. Mostly I was able to relay messages back and forth.

On fine days we sat in the garden, always in the shade of the trees as the sun felt very hot on his head. His head felt vulnerable and we had to be careful we didn't touch him. We took some photos of us together in the garden and one particularly lovely one of him leaning on his hand on the Sunday afternoon, when the treatments were finished.

The hymn book was open on the table and only later, when we had the photo enlarged, could we see that he was studying and making notes of how best to interpret and play, *Oh! Worship the Lord in the Beauty of Holiness.*

The next two days he felt exhausted and stayed in bed studying the Faure Requiem score. His pillow was beginning to be covered in hair and by Wednesday, he had lost so much hair that I collected it in a box and privately kept a curl to put in my locket, but it was dead hair and quite dark compared to his usual gingery and brighter tones.

NanNan went down to *Cwmcidy*, in South Wales for a week to stay with my brother Jim, so I prepared her room for Michael. It was one less flight of stairs to climb and he would be near us should he need us in the night.

Thursday, he was practically bald with a few wispy strands of hair here and there but his beard was not affected and remained completely full all the time. Although he didn't feel like getting out of bed, he was eating well and full of quiet joy.

After lunch I took up a tray of tea and we lingered over it. He said he had spent a wonderful morning with the Lord. He had Casandra's bible and lots of notes in tiny and sometimes indecipherable writing and several other books around him. We spoke of Truth and how it was such a main concern of his.

I remembered how the numbers 85–10 had come into my mind those four years before when he and Casandra had been so close at Canford. On looking up the only thing that made sense with such numbers, I found Verse 10 in Psalm 85 – *Mercy and Truth have met together*, in Casandra there had been a shining Truth.

He went to wash, came back and sat in the chair at the window, I put a rug over his knees. "The trembling has started in my arm," he said.

It was the first time for three weeks, and then he said the feeling was moving up into his head. His arm and hand began to shake, I held him close, cradled his head on my shoulder and talked to him. I had to prevent his head from banging backwards, but I seemed strong enough. The fit spread all over his body, he was shaking uncontrollably, his legs and feet were in a distorted position, his feet pointing inwards. His eyes remained open and I went on talking to him saying it was alright, I had him close.

After a few minutes it began to subside, I could sense it and told him it was passing. He groaned that his right leg was caught, it was pressed against the side of the bed. I tried to ease it but he was a dead weight and as the fit stopped he was inert and exhausted. After a few minutes I dragged the chair nearer the bed and managed to roll him on to it, covering him with a blanket, then I went to the phone and asked for an emergency doctor as it was outside surgery hours.

A doctor came within fifteen minutes, he examined Michael and heard the reason for the occurrence and said that he would best be in hospital for a proper check-up. There was a strike on that day by ambulance drivers so he said if we could get to

Northwick Park ourselves we would save a lot of time. Carol Bellringer was at home across the road, a nurse, so she came and helped me get Michael down the stairs. His leg was very bad, the muscles all seemed tensed and he could hardly stand on it. She drove us into Northwick Park after I had put a few things into a bag and made sure I had my key.

It was a warm summer day, Michael walked or shuffled out of the house in his slippers, pyjamas and dressing gown and the big woolly coat I'd knitted for him. He jokingly chatted with Carol as we sat together in the back of the car.

We arrived at Casualty where two separate doctors examined him and pronounced his heart fit, but there was some feeling lost in his right leg. We had to wait awhile for arrangements to be made in Fleming Ward. He was lying on a hospital trolley almost unperturbed and while we were alone I said, "They told us the treatment might make you worse before you were better, didn't they!"

"Thank you for always being there", he said.

I managed to get a cup of tea for us both and then Dr. Mark Kissin came in. "We are all ready for you upstairs", he said with a smile and told us that they would probably have to step up the amount of drugs – anyway he was in the best place.

Michael's face and head were a bright sunburnt pink and of course, he had a bald pate. He and Mark grinned and talked of the best A.l. wig.

Finally two nurses came and wheeled the trolley through the corridors to the lift, they pushed Michael's trolley bed in beside another but when we reached the ward, Level 6, they had the utmost difficulty wrenching the two apart, much to our amusement. Fleming Ward greeted Michael with open arms, "I've turned up like a bad penny," he said, "Here I am again."

One little nurse smiled and said, "How lovely."

This time he was in a bay, on his own. They settled him into bed but relaxing back he grimaced as he couldn't get his head comfortable against the hospital pillows. "Shall I ask if I can bring in your soft pillows from home?"

"Please", he whispered, so I told him I would go back and fetch a few more things and some clothes. Sister said I could bring a pillow. I ran most of the way home and back again. The familiar soft pillow worked wonders and he felt more comfortable.

I stayed with him until nearly 9 o'clock, he expounded on the scripture he'd been reading that morning of the Holy Spirit and said how amazing it was that the Holy Spirit was mentioned in the New Testament so much yet there were many times when the Holy Spirit wasn't even thought about. After Christ was risen and ascended into heaven, it was the Holy Spirit that came to give strength to the disciples. The Spirit was with us too, ever since, if only we were open to receive Him!

I thanked Michael for teaching me, and he was quite shocked and taken aback, "I can't teach you," he said, "you have taught me so much. It's a sharing. Christians should always get together and talk of their faith, that is how we feed each other – daily bread means sharing the scriptures as well as taking Communion."

I left him, walking home slowly I was very tired but I knew he was in expert hands. The nurses and doctors were a marvellous team, but oh! how I hoped he would not have another fit. Ray came in at 10, I told him and he sank back into a chair in the kitchen. As he listened he was full of sadness that he hadn't been at home with me – that was Thursday, June 18th.

We rang the hospital first thing every morning to find out how he was and we spent hours with him. He was very drugged and sleeping most of the time but on the Saturday morning and again on Sunday he'd had convulsions. The last was very severe, it had continued for twenty minutes and the nurses told us that he had been conscious all the time. It was discovered that he had also suffered a stroke. The whole of his right side was without use or feeling. His right hand was quite limp, his speech was slightly slurred and sometimes he had difficulty finding the right words.

The physiotherapist came up to Fleming and fitted a bar over the bed so that he could lift himself up with his left hand and meantime the drugs were reduced. Mark told us that probably he would have no more fits as there had obviously been a bleeding on the left side of his brain where the most pressure had been. He said, "I doubt whether Michael will ever be able to play the piano again and he knows this."

Did I hear him say that?

He was sleeping a great deal, but when awake he seemed completely to accept the situation.

The physio came every day to stand him on his feet and said we had to keep exercising his hand, otherwise it would begin to waste very quickly. Every minute we were there after that we were continually massaging and moving his fingers up and down and apart, whether he was awake or not. Only four days after the stroke the feeling was back in his leg and he woke up once and thanked me for exercising his hand. "How did you know I was doing it?" I asked him.

For a moment he thought and then smiled, "I could feel it!" he said.

The next day when we arrived in his room, he waved his hand in the air, already able to control it in small movements and even to scratch his beard. I phoned Norman Taylor and told him everything including the fact that the doctors had said he wouldn't be able to play again, I also said that I was sure Michael would love to see him and was it possible for him to come. He replied that he and Mary would drive up next day. When Michael heard, he seemed very relaxed and glad that he was coming.

We all met in the room together and he asked us to stay. He told Norman he was full of regret with his life and relationships, he was full of remorse. Ray and I could hardly believe what he was saying, it was so alien to the person we thought we knew. Norman said, "Then I will give you Absolution! Christ has taken all our sins upon himself, on the Cross, your sins are all forgiven." Then the wonderful words of the Absolution and the sign of the Cross on his head. Michael wept and turned his head from side to side as relief flooded his face.

"Now you will be well," said Norman, "and as to your hand, nobody knows for sure what you will be able to achieve, leave it to God and the Holy Spirit."

Michael said, "Perhaps it is to show me that I need to turn from what I have been doing so far, I have had Ordination on my mind for some time."

Norman replied that God had been nudging and prodding him for ten years before he finally accepted that he was supposed to become a priest. We all prayed together in loving warmth and friendship. Norman told us that a special prayer group had been formed to pray for us and for Michael's healing. They returned home and every day we phoned them to tell them how we were.

Many times I felt the presence of an Angel with us. I had known it for the first time when, just before the Radio Therapy treatment started, we had a really gigantic storm in the night which lasted for several hours. It was entirely exhilarating to me and afterwards Michael had said he had felt the same. I had the idea, how could we worry about a small electrical beam directed at Michael's head when the great electrical discharges in the sky were so vast and all around us?

It was then that I had the vision of a huge Angel seated on our roof. Again in hospital I felt the presence of one, near the bed, I thought of it as a sign of Michael's healing, but later I realised that it must have been an Angel of Death coming gently to take Michael across, the greater healing anyway.

One afternoon he said that he wished I could be there at night, it was always so long and less bearable than the days, when he seemed to sleep such a lot. I asked Sister if it was possible and she answered immediately "Of course you can stay, whenever you like."

We were amazed, but accepted it as another sign of the Holy Spirit working in everyone. Ray and I arranged that he should spend his time there during the day when I would sleep, then I would go during the evening and stay until Michael was given his breakfast.

For the first few nights I had two armchairs on which to rest. Then a bed was brought in so that I could lie down comfortably some of the time. Michael was very glad I was there. The staff were in short supply during the night – only two nurses to look after the whole Ward. One evening I overheard two very young nurses in conversation down the corridor, "I'm not at all surprised he wants his Mum with him, I needed my Mum with me when I had the flu!"

Sometimes if a patient pressed a bell for attention, it took a while for a nurse to answer it. So whenever Michael needed more Disprin, I would just walk along to the desk to collect them. He needed cool cloths on his head to ease the ache and heat which he was still feeling and he needed to sit up quite often to change his position. A large walking frame was given to him and although it was difficult, he did manage to get across to the toilet with my help. His right leg and foot were progressing and he seemed to want to exercise them as much as possible.

There was often a male nurse on duty who came to help me sometimes, but most often we managed together. Michael said, "It is good to have you here, I can only say thank you Mummy."

I said that Ray and I were very conscious of the night that Christ was praying and asked the disciples to watch and pray but they had always fallen asleep when He returned to them. I told Michael that we were watching and praying and would be with him all the while.

During the day Ray took letters in for him to read and dictate the replies. They did a lot of work for the Milton Abbey Festival, but time was passing, it was the end of June and Michael realised that he wouldn't be well enough to return to work for several months.

"You had better cancel all my future engagements", he told Ray.

I can't imagine what this statement must have meant to him. The conducting of the Milton Abbey Festival would have been a supreme experience; then came the question of taking up the Rochester appointment!

One day a new doctor came to see him who was, in his own words, 'the one who treated the whole man.' He came quite late one evening so I was there, and left them alone to talk. They discussed the possibility of him coming home, with perhaps him being in a wheelchair, how his work could go on, how after several weeks they would take him home to see how he could cope, at first for short stays and how Michael could ask Rochester to manage for a while without him.

"They won't be unsympathetic employers surely", he said "and you could postpone your appointment for a few months."

Michael was so much brighter after this visit and said, "I can see I shall have to work hard at my hand."

But already he was beginning to do his own finger exercises and played with his good hand on the upright piano in the day room, showing the physio what sort of specialist exercises he would need. The doctors were astonished, they said it was miraculous that after such a short time since the stroke, there was so much movement. They were usually greatly rewarded if there was slight movement after a month.

I arrived at the hospital one evening before Ray had left so that we should be together. Michael sat propped against his pillows and talked for about an hour, all about his visit to Chicago. The excitement of the skyscrapers and the view from the top of the 1,300 ft. Sears Tower, his visit to the Exchange where herds of cattle and fields of wheat were all changing hands, with nothing physically moving except the money. The atmosphere of the huge young country, how the people, so expansive in one way but brash and rude and uncivil in other ways and how wonderful it had been to return home to find courtesy again from strangers. It was a wonderful pouring out of his experiences to us, we didn't dare break it in case we interrupted and spoilt the flow.

I took NanNan in to see him on her return from Wales. It was very hot in the ward that afternoon and whilst sitting beside him she gently slid to the floor in a faint. A nurse came but my Mother was already coming round. Michael was worried for her, but there were many times when she had fainted before and would do so again. Later he asked me how she was and suddenly could not say NanNan so he called her Mrs. Barton, I smiled and assured him she was alright.

One morning a representative from the Blandford Choral Society came to see him. Debbie Armstrong-Beech brought two beautiful parting gifts from the choir, a small silver tray and glass goblet, both inscribed, *With appreciation from the Blandford Choral Society 1975–1981.* Michael was not really well enough that day to fully realise the journey that Debbie had made and the love she had brought from all the choir for his recovery and success in his new job at Rochester. We heard later how much they were all going to miss him and how much wonderful music they had shared with him, under his direction.

On July the 3rd his left side wasn't so strong; during the night he had found it very difficult to use the frame to get across the room. The pulley over his head for his left hand didn't seem to be of any use and sitting at the edge of the bed he could hardly remain upright, it was all I could do to hold him. Many times he tried to ease his bladder only to soil the bed and each time the nurses changed the sheets he told them how sorry he was. They cheerfully grinned at him and never at any time did they make him feel any loss of dignity. They were charming, loving and always explained what they were going to do even though he looked asleep when the time came to take his blood pressure yet again.

Ray said he thought Michael wasn't so well and I agreed, for him to be weakening on his left side now, meant it was more difficult to move him to relieve pressure points. We were often massaging his muscles, a shoulder or a leg and once or twice his leg would be seized with severe cramp. It was an obvious agony and we had to get his leg out of bed and put his foot to the floor to ease it. To have cramp meant that the feeling was returning more and more to his limbs, this was encouraging and he had less heat in his head.

Then came a small miracle, his hair was beginning to grow again, little wisps appearing here and there and his beard was as strong and bushy as it had ever been.

That weekend Mark came in with a team of doctors and looked at Michael sleeping. As he roused to smile at them, his eyes could hardly focus on Mark's face. "How are you today?"

"Not as good since I lost my balance", he replied. His eyes kept rolling upwards though he tried to hold them steady.

Mark told us outside the room that he thought Michael had suffered another stroke, this time he called it Petit Mal.

Ray and I went to St. John's Church for communion that

Sunday morning before returning to the hospital. That night Michael slept longer in between his needs for Disprin. I dozed and woke with a start to realise that it was nearly 7 a.m. We were usually awake earlier than that. I went to Michael's side, he was lying with his head very much on one side, he said in a fumbling way that he needed a bottle. I replied that he would have to press his bell for a nurse. I put the buzzer in his hand but his fingers didn't have the strength to press. For the first time Michael saw me weep there beside him.

He looked at me searchingly and whispered, "Is NanNan alright?"

I said yes, she was fine. "You are going to be alright," I told him, "God's arms are so much stronger than mine."

He said, "I am going to be in absolute bliss."

I put his arm around my neck and we stayed close for a little while.

"Don't go," he whispered.

"No, of course not, I'll go and ring Daddy to come in."

The nurses came to wash him and I telephoned Ray from the Ward. "Is he not so good?" he asked.

"You're right, darling," I said, "he is dying."

From that moment we both stayed in the hospital. On Tuesday Norman and Mary returned, we said prayers together, finishing with Psalm 23. As we reached the last few lines, Michael joined in and said it with us, a wonderful moment while we all held hands.

The nurses had said that it might be quite a few days before he died but I knew it wouldn't be long and told them what I felt. Wednesday he seemed unconscious but we held his hands and went on talking and praying, not knowing if he would be aware of us or how much he would hear. Sometimes a small movement of his hand would faintly mean he was there.

In the afternoon Clare Cardozo came and sat with us, she stayed until early evening when we persuaded her to return home.

We bathed his eyes continually with small pieces of damp cotton wool and at last managed to keep his eyelids closed. When we tried to put his head a little more comfortably on the pillow he gave a little cry. Sister said he must have an injection because he was feeling pain. She said it would make his breathing heavier but it would stop him suffering.

We asked Mark not to worry him with tubes and special venous feeds and to allow him to die quietly, so apart from giving him an X-ray that evening just to check that his chest was clear, they agreed. The X-ray showed that his lungs were free from congestion.

His temperature rose to an enormous heat; the nurses changed the bed and placed a basket for his feet and little foam cups for his heels. He lay against his pillow, his breath heavy and even. After the heat came a continuing coldness, his hands were thin and pale, slightly blue and became clammy and damp. His head was damp, too, we dried him carefully with warm cloths.

About twenty past one in the morning an unmistakable slight difference occurred in his breathing. I said, "He is going, it won't be long." We held his hands and told him to go. "Don't worry about us" we said, "Go darling boy, go home!" With quiet strength Ray spoke the Lydgate poem from Temple days – *Tarry no Longer*.

We willed him over – his breath was like the sea – there were four or five ordinary breaths then a larger one, a few more small ones, then a gathering of breath and once more a few easy ones. His hands tightened in ours for one moment and with a small breath, he died. Two a.m. Thursday, 9th July. He was so still!

Nurses came to the sound of our bell, also Dr. Yelland. Staff nurse knelt beside the bed and wept. We silently sat there weeping, looking at Michael. His spirit had already left, it was an amazing and wonderful thing to see, there lying against the pillow was now almost an empty husk, the outside of a shell, how mysterious and how Holy.

We left after a little while and stayed the rest of that night in another room. We held each other close and strangely, slept a while. Sister woke us with tea about seven thirty, we dressed and left the hospital. Outside the traffic was streaming past, people were busy, running, shouting, being noisy and full of life – why didn't they know that something momentous had happened, didn't they realise how close to death we all are?

We decided to walk home and prepare ourselves to return later to collect certificates and all the other papers that were needed.

We made arrangements for an undertaker in Wimborne to come and collect Michael the next day from the hospital. We had already decided that the funeral should be in the Minster. Ray had asked him one day if he would like to go back.

We spent a long time phoning – there were so many, arrangements to make and so many people to tell. We were strong and full of the great and wonderful experience it had been, to be with Michael on his great crossing over with such faith, courage and blessing.

The next morning we returned to the hospital, this time to the little chapel room downstairs where the funeral director's assistants had placed him in the coffin. He looked more himself, his head was on a swan's-down pillow and I remember thinking how lovely and soft for his sore head, but knew he didn't need it any more. He was covered in a silky robe. I put my fingers against his cheek, it was like touching a marble statue. We saw the men carry the coffin into their splendid car for the journey to Dorset. Michael was going back to his beloved Dorset, for the last time. We watched the car wend its way round the hospital roads and out into the traffic. We had seen him off and we were actually smiling as we walked home hand in hand.

~·~·~·~·~·~·~

Dorset

Those next few days we were in a sort of "high" when God's purpose is seen to be working very clearly, even though one doesn't fully understand. Much later when a kind of normality returned, the clarity had faded.

How I treasure that clearness, it is just like the most beautiful spring day with everything washed clean by a shower of rain. An edge to every bright colour and a leap of joy from ones own heart at the knowledge of Truth.

Michael wrote several years ago:

> *Recently I flew for the first time, I wept with the Holy Spirit, as above the purity of the clouds and with a clean and beautiful view of the world below, impossibly far below, I felt utterly close to God. His perception is surely such a view of life, no other sense but beauty.*

This was how we felt and how we managed to get through those first days and weeks.

There were so many letters to write, phone calls to make, and on the telephone we had to warn each other not to sound too joyful for the sake of the person hearing us at the other end of the line. Indeed we were often told, "How strong you sound, how can you sound so strong?" We could only repeat that it was Michael's strength and faith and now we had it also. In Corrie ten Boom's books, she says that God gives you the strength when it is needed and not before and we know that to be true.

We were also upheld by the great wealth of letters written to us, letters of love and faith, so full of warmth and sympathy. The letters were overwhelming from the Cathedral at Rochester expressing the sadness they felt at the loss of one who would have been their future colleague. Barry Ferguson wrote:

Michael was one of the most complete people I have met. Faith in God and Jesus Christ permeated everything: his care for people, his wide interest, his sensitivity and generosity. Michael saw into the heart of things, saw the goodness of things, and hence came his sense of joy and fun. Even in his illness it seems that he never lost his vision that in God everything would be well. This is faith in action, inspiring to see.

We left NanNan with my sister, together in the house at Harrow on the Hill and went to Wimborne by coach. The Minster Governors had given us Michael's house, 'for as long as we needed it', we stayed there for two months. But first the ordeal of the funeral lay ahead.

Our first few hours at 8 Minster View were warmed and softened by a visit from Mrs. Phyllis Saville with a huge bunch of sweet peas for us. Her love and concern were echoed by so many friends and colleagues of Michael, we were only just beginning to find out how much he was loved and how much he had inspired his pupils and the community. Yet we must have realised, for during those weeks in hospital he had talked so much with the nurses and had carried on a kind of Ministry there, his faith was a shining example. It was strange and sadly wonderful, to be in the house surrounded by all his things. It was such a short while since we had been there sorting out his music and work.

The day of the funeral arrived, July 20th.

At 2 o'clock we walked into the Minster to see the coffin already there, standing on the blue carpet under the central tower. Our flowers and the F.R.C.O. Hood were placed on it.

To our astonishment the Minster was full, afterwards it was reported that over 450 people were present, including Dr. George Thalben-Ball and other Temple friends, relations, London friends, Jürgen Schwab from Stuttgart and the Minster congregation who had heard Michael playing the organ for seven years. Barry Ferguson was there from Rochester to play the organ for the service, Edmund Buxton was to help the team of clergy and Martin Marriott of Canford gave the address We were amazed at the sound of the singing. We had chosen for the first hymn, *All my hope on God is founded*, written by Herbert Howells on the death of his own son, Michael. The sound of the voices lifted us and sustained us throughout the whole service. The choir sang a hymn to a tune that Michael had composed and then Martin Marriott gave the address:-

> *The news of Michael's death must surely have affected all of us who count ourselves as his friends, in much the same way. Reactions of sheer unbelief, deep sadness and probably a feeling of waste that such a loving and*

creative life should have been cut short so early in its course; all so difficult for us to absorb, let alone understand or accept.

Many of you will have known him better and longer than I, and you will all have your own private memories of him and reasons to be grateful for his life. I would not wish to intrude upon those private thoughts. However, I do gladly and humbly accept this opportunity to recall publicly my own thoughts about him, in the hope that by so doing, we may all be enabled to concentrate our thinking about him for a few minutes and to give thanks to God together for his life and for his contribution to our own lives.

Certainly for the five years that I have known him and of course for many years longer than that it would be quite impossible to talk about Michael except in terms of music and his Christian belief. One or other or both of those elements were present in everything he did, everything he thought, everything he was. Those are the only terms in which I know how to interpret his life and personality. That most important ingredient of his being, his ability to love, from which so many of us benefited so greatly, was the direct expression of those twin elements.

All of us remember clearly, indeed vividly, the marvellous warm and gentle quality of his friendship, whether or not we had the capacity to respond to it in similar terms. His was a friendship that was shot through with fun and light, which enriched our lives whatever our individual relationship with him may have been, particularly happy for me are the memories of him sitting in our kitchen chatting to the family, his infectious giggle, and his accounts of his somewhat hazardous journeys in Sidney, his elderly car – which also seemed to live almost entirely by faith.

Surely the most eloquent testimony of our feelings for him is the presence of so many of his friends here today, especially when you know that amongst this congregation are his beloved Dr. Thalben-Ball of the Temple Church, his nurses from London, his friend all the way from Stuttgart and many others from various parts of the country. It was of course, in the world of music that he was at his most active, ardent and enthusiastic – whether as a chorister in the Temple choir, at school, at University, at Canford or here in the Minster.

He shared his knowledge, his skill and his perception with others in a most generous way, teaching pupils of all ages and ability with equal concern and happiness; training choirs at Canford and Blandford or here, with great sensitivity, planning and organising concerts and recitals in a seemingly endless stream, taking much of the donkey work upon himself.

But his first love, his true love, I feel, was to perform himself. This is what really lit him up and made vibrant his body, mind and spirit. He would work endless hours, (not always in the most organised way, it should be said) he would try to pack more than was humanly possible into most days, much as if he sensed that he had but a limited time for this life's work. He loved to accompany other musicians and showed us his very delicate musical skills in the process.

I particularly remember a wonderful recital he organised

and gave with several friends in the dining hall at Canford some four years ago and his superb performance of Schubert's piano sonata here in the Minster and this year – his Annus Mirabilis – in every sense crammed full of activity with his recitals in Chicago and Stuttgart, achieving his F.R.C.O. and his very remarkable performance, again here in the Minster of Messiaens Transport de Joie which he played on Ascension Day – the last occasion on which he played here and which we will hear again most appropriately, at the end of the service.

If his music was his most important means of expressing himself, his Christian belief was his mainspring, the source of his love, his creativity and his enduring courage. We saw it expressed in so many ways, but I particularly treasure those all too brief occasions when he tried to explain to me – a non musician – the subtle way in which a piece of music expressed the spiritual content of the words that were being sung. He had, I thought, a rare gift in discerning the importance of words in prose, in poetry and music and never more so than in sacred works. He could be quite overwhelmed by the combination of words and music as they expressed so sublimely his own deep religious feeling and understanding. It was why he so loved his work here and was so looking forward to Rochester – spending his days making music in a Christian setting.

It is illuminating to know that even in the last days of his life he was working on the Dream of Gerontius and the Faure Requiem in order that he might be able the better, to communicate their meaning to his performers. How glad we must all be, deep down, that his belief was so strong and so real to him, that he could go through his illness with such sincere acceptance, and face his own death open eyed; his main concern being not for himself but for his parents. We do not understand why the God in whom he trusted so truly, should call him so early – but we must try and learn from Michael and accept as he did. What profound lessons there are here for us.

We need not be sad for Michael for in his own words he has found endless bliss! We can but be relieved that he has been released from his illness, but our hearts go out to his parents who, more than any of us, will feel his loss. We would like them to know that they have our love, compassion and friendship.

So we thank God for Michael's life, for his love, his friendship, his musicality and for the way he shared that music with so many and above all for the fact that on his pilgrimage through life and from life to the life hereafter, he had such a deep and trusting faith in God. That thought reminded me – as it may also remind some of you – of that most evocative passage at the end of Pilgrim's progress, where Mr. Standfast crosses the river to meet his Lord. I hope you may feel that it is appropriate for Michael.

When Mr. Standfast had thus set things in order and the time being come for him to haste away, he also went down to the river.

Now there was a great calm at that time in the river; wherefore Mr. Standfast when he was about halfway in, stood a while and talked to his companions that had waited upon him thither, and he said, "This river has been a terror to many, yea the thoughts of it also have often frightened me. But now methinks, I stand easy, my foot is fixed upon that which the feet of the priests that bare the ark of the covenant stood. The thoughts of what I am going to and of the conduct that waits for me on the other side, doth lie as a glowing coal at my heart."

Now while he was thus in discourse, his countenance changed, his strong man bowed under him and after he had said, "Take me, for I come unto Thee," he ceased to be seen of them. But, glorious it was to see how the open region was filled with trumpeters and pipers, with singers and players on stringed instruments to welcome the Pilgrim on the other side, at the beautiful gate of the City.

Then we heard the Messiaen, *Transports de Joie* played by Barry. Michael had told a colleague once who declared he couldn't understand Messiaen compositions, "If you have the opportunity to be alone at night in a darkened Cathedral, then you will understand his music."

We needed no darkened Cathedral, darkness was deep inside us – a darkness that even so was surrounded by light, and we understood.

A vivid memory I have of that day is of the Reverend Barney Hopkinson standing in the cemetery, his surplice flying in the breeze, his arms outstretched, saying, what is one of my most favourite prayers from the Eucharist,

Father of all, we give you thanks and praise, that when we were still far off you met us in your Son and brought us home. Dying and living, he declared your love, gave us grace and opened the gate of glory.

May we who share Christ's body live his risen life; we who drink his cup bring life to others; we whom the Spirit lights give light to the world.

Keep us firm in the hope you have set before us, so we and all your children shall be free, and the whole earth live to praise your name; through Christ our Lord. Amen.

The memories crowd in; Edmund and Katharine telling us of their visit to their Godson who gave *them* joy and peace and strength as they sat beside his bed. The supper given us by Judith and Martin for our guests, one of whom was Suzanne Platau, the young violinist. She and Michael had given several recitals of violin sonatas over the past two years. Then there was the joy we felt for Michael. Later I was to worry and tease myself over the contradiction of that joy and our anguish and sorrow, until I realised Christ was sorrowing with us. But I felt that Michael was carrying on his work in some way, some greater work, and that those three young ones who had gone so early – first Casandra, then Christopher and now Michael, joined in love and friendship on Earth, were now joined in praise and worship in Heaven.

I had some wonderful dreams and often felt that Michael was close. He wrote once, that physical existence was a vehicle for our souls in which the growing awareness of God and love would find expression in our journey through life; death must be met with the journey well advanced, so that in release from the limits of physical existence, the soul can surpass all earthly understanding and yet be in communion with souls on Earth too.

Sometimes I found myself so close to Michael I could touch his hand on my shoulder. I could hear him say, "It's so lovely to see you both, what is important is to see and do everything clearly and beautifully while you are there, you will need all that experience for here!"

My first dream was seeing Michael come for me, taking my hand and lifting me up from my bed, looking down I saw Ray and myself still sleeping. We flew, or what seemed to me like flying, over coloured ground all flowers and hills, he said, "It's glorious!" and appeared larger and larger though leaving me to go far away, "Go back and look after Daddy", he said, and I found myself back in bed.

In another dream we were standing either side of a barred gate looking happily at each other and then I was aware that we were very tiny compared to a vast throne which reached up in immensity with a shining figure above. We gazed and gazed, Michael one side of the gate and me on the other but very close. How deeply meaningful are now the words:

> *Therefore with Angels and Archangels and with all the company of Heaven we laud and magnify thy glorious name, evermore praising thee and saying, Holy, Holy, Holy, Lord God of Hosts, Heaven and Earth are full of thy Glory, Glory be to thee Oh! Lord most High.*

In August at the Milton Abbey Festival of which he would have been the Director, they performed the Faure Requiem and just as he would have wanted, indeed had said, that no performance of the Requiem should ever be given unless it was dedicated to someone's memory; it was dedicated to Michael as part of the Mass. We sat with Judith and Martin Marriott and our hearts lifted with the music at the final movement of Paradise.

We walked out of the Abbey into that glorious view, the sun setting in a great red golden blaze of harvest time, a smoky haze from the stubble fires drifting across and enhancing the dramatic colour. Then the stars began to appear as we motored back to Wimborne, so numerous and so large they seemed just above our heads. In my heart I held a star close and it comforted me.

Michael's colleagues and friends and particularly Michael Bartlett, a member of the Minster choir and a Governor of the Minster and Edward Monds, a solicitor and also a Governor, had talked to us from the first days of their thoughts. Surely some sort of music trust must be established? Michael's work of inspiring the young people he'd taught, conducted, accompanied and above all the inspiration he'd shown whilst playing the organ for the Minster services, couldn't just stop!

When I thought of the power that had come from his hands and feet whilst playing, his whole body and soul deep in the music, my heart wept at the silence and stillness of him in death, but we had found a poem, printed on a card amongst his papers, an anonymous poem which today one sees quite often, but at that particular time in 1981 was quite new to us. Michael had obviously found it and we read it at just the right moment:

If I should die and leave you here awhile
Be not like others sore, undone, who keep
Long vigils by the silent dust and weep.
For my sake turn again to life and smile
Nerving thy heart and trembling hand, to do,
Something to comfort other hearts than thine.
Complete these dear unfinished tasks of mine,
And I, perchance, may therein comfort you.

Somehow we gathered strength and purpose, though it was with more than a trembling hand with which we turned to life and set to work to complete his unfinished tasks.

The Michael James Music Trust was registered in the Autumn of 1981 with the Charity Commissioners by Edward Monds, our treasurer. Michael Bartlett became the administrator and with Reverend Norman Taylor and Christopher Grundy, a friend from Temple, we agreed to form the trustees.

Money flowed in from many sources, enough in the first year to provide book prizes for young choristers. The inaugural concert was given in St. Michael's Church, Cornhill, in the City of London by Sir George Thalben-Ball, with the choir directed by Jonathan Rennert, solo instrumentalists and singers. The music was by Bach, Parry and Walford Davis. We then organised concerts to raise funds and within a very short time we were able to award our first organ scholarship at Rochester Cathedral.

The Trust benefitted from a generous grant from the newly formed Foundation for Sport and the Arts, making us more widely known. It has grown beyond our expectations, assisting young musicians of great talent throughout the country. There is an annual award winner's concert each spring in the Minster.

The objects of the Trust are: the education of music and especially the encouragement of music performed in a Christian setting for the enrichment of worship.

From those very small beginnings, giving book prizes to Choristers at the Temple, the Minster and Rochester Cathedral, the Trust has grown to the point of having four organ scholars and of helping young musicians to reach their potential which, perhaps without our help, they would not attain.

I am often asked to give a luncheon talk, or after dinner speech, about myself and the aims and achievements of the Trust. I am so grateful for all my early training and experience in the theatre which is helpful on such occasions. It allows me to include experiences of working with famous actors, add a few anecdotes, and complete the story with our life now. It is a very pleasant way in which to help to raise funds.

Sometimes during a service when the music really does enrich the whole congregation with that extra sense of being close to God, I would find myself smiling with the love I'd known when Michael was alive.

One morning, at just such a moment, I heard him say, "I'm very close Mummy, I can only come to you when you are feeling happy for me." He 'stayed' throughout the whole service. That sense of closeness and of him being with us has come to me many times. That he is living in quite another way from us but still 'living', is something of which I am completely assured; that he loves us as we love him and that he must be supremely happy and full of gladness fills me with confidence for the future.

The Reverend Michael Stancliffe, one time Dean of Winchester, wrote:

> ... that making is the everlasting occupation of those in whose midst God dwells. What do they make? Literally they make Him great; that is, they "magnify Him" (a Rochester memory of – "We don't magnify the Lord enough!"). "Nowadays magnifying generally suggests using a lens to help us see what is small for our unaided eyes. But when the word first entered the vocabulary of religion – as when Mary magnified the Lord, and the

Psalmist bids us "praise the Lord with me, and let us magnify His name together", Psalm 34.3, in that original sense it means "to speak or act for the honour and glory of God" – to act be it noted, as well as to speak. So making – is the ceaseless occupation of the whole company of Heaven, each doing his utmost to honour God by creating a celebration of God's glory. It is commonly symbolised in terms of music, with voices, harps and trumpets, but we may surely believe that the artist and craftsman in every human soul will have, in Heaven, the opportunity to magnify the Lord in whatever medium he or she is most skilled.

Reflecting on Kipling's poem, "When Earth's last picture is painted", he imagines that we shall "splash at a ten league canvas with brushes of comet's hair" and the poem ends:

> *And only the Master shall praise us,*
> *and only the Master shall blame.*
> *And no one shall work for money,*
> *and no one shall work for fame,*
> *But each for the joy of working,*
> *and each in his separate star,*
> *Shall draw the Thing as he sees It,*
> *for the God of Things as They are!*

Little by little and sometimes not so little but with a great stride, we move on and learn, I think we are given small pieces of a giant jigsaw puzzle and I wait patiently for them, to fit them into place.

I had a dream that I was crawling across dark muddy ground that slowed my progress, but ahead were several bright discs or coins and as I reached them, picked them up one at a time, after the fifth one Michael's hand was there and lifted me up out of the mud.

Every day there are so many choices to make, so many things 'we have done or not done'. I meditated clearly one morning that I was only human and could do no other than continue to try and with God's help I must forgive myself, then accept completely the words of the Absolution. A great flood of forgiveness came over me, an overwhelming warmth of God's forgiveness and I found myself picking up the first bright coin of my dream.

The following Christmas Ray bought me a small telescope. He said that he had always known how interested I had been in looking at the stars and planets but that it was also a symbol of looking outwards from our sorrow. It was a wonderful gift and what magic I felt when setting it up for the moon to sail across, to see the craters and plains, the mountains clear and bright and the awe of seeing it gently floating out of view. The planets I can see as little circles as the magnification doesn't allow me to see any detail, the stars are just points of light, but just staring into the skies with a little more clarity gives wings to my mind! Wasn't it Plato who said that "Music gives a soul to the Universe, wings to the mind, flight to the imagination, a charm for sadness and leads to all that is good, just and beautiful." I could watch those amazing skies and listen to the music of the spheres with my heart.

My mother's arms were a wonderful solace those first years, her lap for my head, my tears making her skirt damp and her tears falling on my hair. They were a precious few years for she gradually depended on me to look after her more and more. She died just before reaching her 92nd birthday. Two weeks before, I had lifted her hand to my head and she moved her fingers in my hair and fondled the back of my neck as she had when I was a child, I knew that was our farewell. We buried her ashes in the churchyard of St. Mary's on the Hill at Harrow. The spire shows for miles and Michael had said he loved to catch the first glimpse of it on a drive home.

There was only one more year before Ray would have to retire from teaching at the Guildhall, so we decided that at last we could move to Wimborne, to take on the responsibilities of Administrators of the Trust, for Michael Bartlett had become ordained and would soon be moving on to a parish of his own. Wimborne had been calling us for some while with so many friends, so many lovely memories round every corner. Such a small town with beautiful country to the north and west and Michael's grave in the cemetery on the hill; we had found a phrase that seemed to sum up his life, and with his name, dates, and his letters after his name, we had written on the gravestone, *All his soul with music offered.* The urge sometimes to be there was very strong and Dorset seemed a long way away.

We put our Edwardian house in Harrow up for sale and within a week it was sold, at least we were in negotiations with a young couple who loved it from the moment they came to see it. I travelled down to Wimborne staying for a week in a guest house to look for something suitable. I saw over a dozen properties, some so unsuitable as to be a pain to even begin to look at, but three quite lovely in different ways. Ray joined me as soon as he could get away and we decided on the house where we now live.

Our house is on a steep hill above the town close to the country lanes and from our windows we can see the other side of the town and fields and country beyond. A very new house, warm and comfortable, such a change from the Edwardian house but still with character and a small enclosed garden. Beyond, three great oak trees. The road had been a footpath and track where we had walked with Michael picking blackberries, a hilly field not far from Minster View, but now a cul-de-sac with several houses.

It was home right from the start of our new life and we were welcomed with open arms into the congregation of the Minster. The wonderful delight we felt when occasionally someone would say, "Oh! are you Michael's parents? I knew him well", and then off he or she would go into a warm, friendly or loving anecdote, small things remembered with such affection that our hearts were filled with contentment.

We had realised more and more how much he had been loved and over the years we now know the inspirational nature of his faith; to think of him is to find a wholeness, a full circle. The calm baby, the small boy who would sometimes surprise us with his wise sayings, the developing musician and Christian, the friend and teacher and that glorious looking forward at his own death – how can we not be happy for him? How can we not have come to terms with our loss; not to get over the loss, oh! no! never while we live, but to learn to live with it – we find we have "garlands instead of ashes, oil of gladness to mingle with our tears and garments of splendour for our heavy hearts."

Perhaps the most powerful dream I have had, not long ago, I was entirely aware of Michael being in my arms. I couldn't ask how or, trembling, why he was there, holding him as gently and as closely as I dared for fear of breaking this gift of Grace and the joyous light that seemed to be surrounding us. I looked into his face and he seemed to be the same, yet much more, I knew that we had shared the grief of his going. A parting that was just a long drawn breath for him in God's time but all 'the years for us since we had held his hands and let him go. Together, we seemed to share a deep smile of joy and sorrow for each other; in his eyes, I glimpsed the glory! Heaven must be this light, this joyous light and God's love, our shared love was why we could still be together. At the fading of the vision – dream – I knew that it would give me Life to live until I, too, die and on and on!

Now there is a great deal of work for us to do with the Trust. So many young people giving their lives to their music, so dedicated and talented, they deserve every bit of help the Trust can give. They go to special master classes, or courses; we can supply travelling expenses abroad, help with college fees, sponsor concerts and recitals and give as much encouragement as we can. In return, the award winners give recitals or concerts in aid of the Trust so that every year there is an event in some part of the country every month or so.

In 1991, the 10th Anniversary year, Dame Gillian Weir, C.B.E. gave a recital in the Minster. Before she played she said, "Knowing how thin a veil separates those who have gone on, from those of us who've loved and still remain, I feel sure Michael is watching this celebration now. He will hear what I play and listen, I hope, not too critically."

Her playing was superb and to a full Minster. We only knew afterwards that she was suffering from bronchitis and was feeling rather ill. The concert was such a success that we were enabled to give two scholarships to the local Queen Elizabeth's School, to further the musical education of a boy and a girl and to make a stronger link between school and Minster.

Trust organ scholars are at the Cathedrals of St. Paul's London, Rochester, Chelmsford, Durham and St. Martin in the Fields. In 1991 we were able to give a grant to one of the first members of the girls' choir introduced at Salisbury Cathedral. They sing for some of the services, they attend the Music School with the boys and will benefit from that marvellous musical education.

Every year in April there is a lunch time recital in Southwark Cathedral given in memory of Michael and that special week long ago when he brought the choir from Durham University to sing for all the services. Many of the recitals have been played by the Cornel Music Group which include Annabelle and Richard Willetts and Richard Hall, friends and colleagues. Dr. Richard Hall is now a Trustee; he was at Durham with Michael and it was there he received his doctorate.

Our gratitude goes out to so many people for all the support they have given, for their confidence that what the Trust does is truly right, but perhaps it is the Bournemouth and District Musicians Christian Fellowship to whom our special love goes. They have arranged a prestigious event annually, to raise money for the Trust, at which the Mayor and Mayoress of Bournemouth are present. It is usually a celebration of the talent of young musicians, so a youth orchestra takes a large part and each year the Highcliffe Junior Choir sing under the superb guidance of their conductor, Mary Denniss M.B.E. She received her award for her services to music, justly deserved, for her training of the children is brilliant, from the youngest at the tender age of eight to the seventeen year olds who she successfully sends on to the music colleges and universities. The response and the warmth at this concert is overwhelmingly full of encouragement, many of the members of the Fellowship knew Michael, and have become our friends, particularly since we moved to Wimborne. Sadly this Fellowship has now ceased to be.

We have put down roots and in time have realized that this is where our roots have always been. We have come to the conclusion that our whole married life has been lived with Dorset at the centre, here we are at last, in full knowledge of the fact, though it has lain as a shadow, deep in our minds always. We have our treasured memories and, by God's grace, they are the treasures of His Glory.

St. Paul writes to the Ephesians:

> *May he grant you strength and power through His Spirit in your inner being, that through faith, Christ may dwell in your hearts in love. With deep roots and firm foundations, may you be strong to grasp with all God's people what is the breadth and length and height and depth of the love of Christ and to know it, though it is beyond knowledge.*

Michael knew it, his inner being was full of faith and since his death our faith has grown.

We live so near the cemetery that we do not feel the need to visit the grave very often, but we keep the stone supplied with flowers and greenery from our garden. We ride up there on our bicycles, on our way to the lanes and a ten mile spin. The hedgerows are beautiful at all times of the year but never more so than in May when the cow parsley stretches for miles and even on the bicycles the white tops are higher than we are. We might pass a car or two but the quiet and sense of peace is profound.

Dorset is a place for deep roots and firm foundations and in the depths of the country there is little change; one can feel the mystery of past people through the ages and the ceaseless rolling seasons. At harvest time the colours of the fields are vibrant; they turn a golden orange and brown, the rolls of straw stretching far to the horizon. Every horizon I see, I am reminded of that famous saying,

> *Life is immortal and love is eternal and death is only an horizon and an horizon is nothing save the limit of one's sight.*

I shall end with a prayer of Michael's written at University.

O Lord Jesus Christ, instil in me the spirit of search with diligence, warmth, integrity, kindness, trustworthiness – love's timeless qualities that guide me to heaven, so that I may earn my reward; infinite love and peace and peaceful rest to infinity, and that I may inspire someone to stop and find this too, give me your help O God.

MICHAEL JAMES

B.A., F.R.C.O. (CHM), A.R.C.M.

1951-1981

"A Mysterious Harmony"

I n 1992, a window in thanksgiving for the life and work of Michael James was installed in the Baptistry of Wimborne Minster.

The window just above the west door was designed by the Dorset stained glass artist, Henry Haig, A.R.C.A. He writes:

The function of stained glass in the Christian context is to be a teaching vehicle of external truths: God's light made manifest. Through colour, tone and line His transmitted energy becoming timeless forms, so revealed, encouraging contemplation towards eternity - to still the viewer, even if only momentarily. Michael James was a musician and teacher of joyous, dynamic creative energy. Through his works he acted as a vehicle for many to express through music the receiving and giving love of God in terms of listening and participation.

The new window is designed to suggest the energy of our Resurrection through the gaining of new life given to us by the act of the Baptism: the first commitment of the soul on its Christian journey. The visual substructure has been evolved from musical notations in terms of intervals and rhythms. From the Baptismal waters flow direct reference from the Dream of Gerontius by Elgar, the work Michael was due to direct but had to leave.

The two inscriptions on either side of the window were designed and carved by Richard Grasby, F.S.D.C., F.R.S.A.

Serve the Lord with gladness
and come before his presence with a song.

Established 1981

Reg. Charity No. 283943

The Michael James Music Trust

Patrons

The Very Revd. John Arnold, Dean of Durham

Dame Janet Baker

Mr. Kenneth Van Barthold

Revd. Preb. Edmund Buxton

Mr. Christopher Dearnley

Lady Beatrix Evison, J.P., B.Sc.

Mr. Barry Ferguson, M.A., F.R.C.O.

Professor David Greer

Sir Michael Hanham, Bart.

Revd. Preb. W. D. Kennedy-Bell

The Rt. Revd. John Kirkham, Bishop of Sherborne

Sir Robin Mackworth-Young, K.C.V.O.

Mr. Martin Marriot, M.A. (Oxon)

Mrs. Judith Marriot

Sir George and Lady Solti

Sir David Willcocks, C.B.E.

Organ Scholarships and Awards

Rochester Cathedral

Durham Cathedral

Chelmsford Cathedral

St. Paul's Cathedral

Southwark Cathedral

St. Martin's in the Fields

Chelsea Old Church

Hampstead Parish Church

City of London School

Canford School

Former Trust Organ Scholars

Now Organists, or Assistants, at cathedrals of:

~ Hereford

~ Norwich

~ Portsmouth

~ Wells

~ Westminster Abbey

~ Worcester

Choristers and Musicians

Durham Cathedral School

Temple Church, London

Girl Choristers at Salisbury and Exeter Cathedrals

Wells Cathedral Music School

Purcell School, Harrow

Annual Grants to University and College Students

Durham University

Royal College of Music

Royal Academy of Music

London College of Music

Guildhall School of Music and Drama

The Birmingham Conservatoire

Queen Elizabeth's School, Wimborne

St. Michael's Church of England School, Colehill, Dorset

Festivals, Concerts, and Sponsorships

Arts Festival Music Workshops sponsored

Concerts promoted:

~ Landemus Choir

~ Highcliffe School Choir

~ Wessex Youth Orchestra

~ South Wessex Junior Singers

Annual Award Winners Concert of Young Professionals, Wimborne

Annual Lunchtime Concert, Southwark Cathedral

Trust sponsored musicians appear in BBC "Young Musician of the Year"

1997: The commissioning of a new work for voices and organ accompaniment.

The Trust is supported by the Foundation for Sport and the Arts.

Discography

Oliver *(soundtrack of the film)*
RCA Victor RB6777

~

Lift Up Your Heads
EMI CLP 3627

~

Makers of History
EMI CLP 1709

~

Music of the Service
EMI CLP 1529

~

Winter Wonderland
EMI TWO 189

~

I Sing Nowell
and
Pat-a-Pan
Philips BF. 1616
Single 45 mono